UT KNOXVILLE LIBRARY

3 9029 00874055 1

D0982622

DATE DUE

Latin American Play Index

Volume 2: 1962-1980

by

HERBERT H. HOFFMAN

The Scarecrow Press, Inc.
Metuchen, N.J., and London
1983

PQ
7082
.D7H63
1983
v. 2

Library of Congress Cataloging in Publication Data

Hoffman, Herbert H.
    Latin American play index.

    1. Latin American drama--Indexes. 2. Latin American
drama--Bibliography. I. Title.
Z1609.D7H63   1983   016.862'008'098   83-8736
[PQ7082.D7]
ISBN 0-8108-1633-4

Copyright © 1983 by Herbert H. Hoffman
Manufactured in the United States of America

Table of Contents

Foreword

In the last twenty years more than 1,700 plays have been published in South America as separate publications or stand-alone works, and as contributions to collections, anthologies, and periodicals. Some of these plays by more than 700 playwrights writing in Spanish, Portuguese, and French are highly charged politically, reflecting the turbulent world that is South America; others are philosophical exercises; many are pure entertainment. Most were written for adults; some for children. Together they constitute a respectable body of literature that ought to attract, for one reason or another, readers everywhere. Latin American Play Index was compiled to facilitate access to this bibliographically somewhat neglected area of world literature.

The present volume, designated volume 2, includes plays published from about 1962 to the present. Volume 1, now in preparation, will be a retrospective volume.

Latin American Play Index covers plays published in four formats. Some appeared as stand-alone works; others were published in collections (defined as books containing several plays by the same author); still others were published in anthologies (defined as books containing plays by different authors); a few, finally, were published in periodicals.

Since all but fourteen of the collections and anthologies covered in Latin American Play Index have previously been mentioned in various volumes of the well-known Handbook of Latin American Studies (HLAS), the HLAS volume and entry numbers have been adopted as reference codes. Only those books coded "00" were not found in HLAS. The complete List of Collections and Anthologies begins on page 113.

For the sake of standardization, Latin American Play Index has adopted the same periodical codes that were introduced by the Handbook of Latin American Studies. Thus, the code UCCH/A stands for the periodical Apuntes of Santiage de Chile. The List of Periodicals Indexed begins on page 129.

Stand-alone plays are described by author, title, and imprint. Throughout, HLAS volume and entry numbers have been added so that readers may easily refer to relevant critical notes and other useful information found in that handbook.

Herbert H. Hoffman

Playwrights Included

Acero, Julio. Mexico.
Acevedo Hernández, Antonio.
  1887. Chile.
Acosta, Ricardo. 1934.
  Venezuela.
Adellach, Alberto. Argentina.
Adoum, Jorge Enrique. Peru.
Agüero Gómez, Gilberto.
  Venezuela.
Aguiar, Claúdio. Brazil.
Aguilera Malta, Demetrio.
  1909. Ecuador.
Aguirre, Isidora. Chile.
Aguirre, Yolanda. Cuba.
Agustín, José. 1944.
  Mexico.
Alban Gomez, Ernesto.
Alberto, Raimundo. Brazil.
Alegría, Alonso. Cuba.
Alencar Pimentel, see
  Pimentel, Altimar de
  Alencar. Brazil.
Aliber, Alicia. Argentina.
Almeida, Abilio Pereira de.
  Brazil.
Almeida, Lyad de. Brasil.
Almeida, Manuel Antônio del.
  Brazil.
Alurista. USA.
Alvarado, Manuel. Luis.
  Argentina.
Alvarado, Rafael. Venezuela.
Alves, Edgard G.. Brazil.
Amado, João Jorge. Brazil.
Amaral, M. A. Brazil.
Amaya Amador, Ramón.
  Honduras.
Anchieta, José de. Brazil.
Andrade, Jorge. Brazil.
Andrade, Oswald de. 1890.
  Brazil.
Andrade Rivera, Gustavo.
  Colombia.
Andreu Iglesias, César.

Aníbal Niño, Jairo.
  Colombia.
Ankerman, Guillermo. Cuba.
Ankerman, Jorge. Cuba.
Antonietto, Elena.
  Argentina.
Arango, Alfredo. Panama.
Arango, Gonzalo. Colombia.
Aranha, José Pereira da
  Graça. Brazil.
Araújo, Alcione. Brazil.
Araujo, Nelson Correia de.
  Brazil.
Arauz, Alvaro. Mexico.
Arce, Manuel José. 1936.
  Costa Rica.
Ardiles Gray, Julio.
  Argentina.
Arellano Guerra, Fausto E.
Arevalo Martinez, Rafael.
  1884.
Argüelles, Hugo. 1932.
  Mexico.
Arinos, Afonso. Brasil.
Arlt, Roberto. 1900.
  Argentina.
Armas y Cárdenas, José de.
  1866. Cuba.
Armijo, Roberto. El Salvador.
Arreola, Juan José. 1918.
  Mexico.
Arriví, Francisco. 1915.
  Puerto Rico.
Arrufat, Antón. 1935. Cuba.
Artiles, Freddy. Cuba.
Assaf, Jesús. Mexico.
Assunçâo, Leilah. Brazil.
Asturias, Miguel Ángel.
  1899. Guatemala.
Athayde, Roberto
  Austregésilo de. 1949.
  Brazil.
Avilés Blonda, Máximo.
  Dominican Republic.

Ayala, Walmir. Brazil.
Azar, Héctor. 1930. Mexico.
Azevedo, Arthur. Brazil.
Azevedo, Manuel Antônio
  Alvares de. Brazil.
Baccaro, Julio. Argentina.
Badía, Nora. 1921. Cuba.
Baez, Edmundo. 1914.
Balla, Andrés. Argentina.
Ballesté, Enrique. Mexico.
Bandrich, Agustín. Mexico.
Barreto, Paulo. 1878. Brazil.
Barros Grez, Daniel. 1834.
  Chile.
Basurto, Luis G. 1920.
Bauer, Luisa. Mexico.
Belaval, Emilio S. 1903.
  Puerto Rico.
Benavente P., David. Chile.
Bender, Ivo. Brazil.
Benedetti, Mario. 1920.
  Uruguay.
Béneke, Walter. 1928. El
  Salvador.
Benítez, Pereira, Ovidio.
  Argentina.
Berrutti, Alejandro E.
  Argentina.
Bethencourt, João. Brazil.
Betti, Atilio. 1922.
  Argentina.
Bezerra Filho, José.
  Brasil.
Bioy Casares, Adolfo. 1914.
  Argentina.
Bivar, Antônio. Brazil.
Blanco, Jorge. Paraguay.
Bloch, Jonas. Brazil.
Bloch, Pedro. Brazil.
Boal, Augusto. Brazil.
Bocanegra, Matías de. 1612.
  Mexico.
Bolón, Hugo. Uruguay.
Bonnin Armstrong, Ana Inés.
  Puerto Rico.
Booi, Hubert.
Borba Filho, Hermilo. 1917.
  Brazil.
Borges, Durval. Brazil.
Borges, José Carlos
  Cavalcanti. Brazil.
Botelho de Oliveira, Manuel.
  Brazil.
Botelho Gosálvez, Rául.
  1917. Bolivia.
Braga, J. Alberto. Brazil.

Brasini, Mário. Brazil.
Brene, José R. Cuba.
Bressan, Lindor. Chile.
Britto García, Luis.
  Venezuela.
Buenaventura, Enrique. 1925.
  Colombia.
Bustillo Oro, Juan. 1904.
  Mexico.
Buttaro, Enrique. Argentina.
Cabrera y Bosch, R. Cuba.
Cabrera y Quintero, Cayetano
  Javier de. Mexico.
Cabrujas, José Ignacio.
  1937. Venezuela.
Caldas, Erasmo Catauli.
  Brazil.
Calderón, Manuel A.
  Argentina.
Calizaya Velásquez, Zenobio.
  Bolivia.
Callado, Antônio. Brazil.
Calvet, Aldo. Brazil.
Calveyra, Arnaldo. Venezuela.
Câmara, Isabel. Brazil.
Camargo, Joracy. 1898.
  Brazil.
Campos, Geir. 1924. Brazil.
Cañas, Alberto F. Costa
  Rica.
Cantón, Wilberto. 1923.
  Mexico.
Carballido, Emilio. 1925.
  Mexico.
Cárdenas, Raúl de. Cuba.
Cardoso, Lúcio. Brazil.
Cardozo, Joaquim Maria
  Moreira. 1897. Brazil.
Carella, Tulio. 1912.
  Argentina.
Carlino, Carlos. 1910.
  Argentina.
Carreño, Virginia.
  Argentina.Carrero,
  Jaime. Puerto Rico.
Carvalho, Antônio C Brazil.
Carvalho, Carlos. Brazil.
Carvalho, Hélio. Brazil.
Carvalho, Hermínio Bello de.
  Brazil.
Casali, Renzo. Argentina.
Castellanos, Rosario. 1925.
  Mexico.
Castellanos de Ríos, Ada.
  Bolivia.

Castillo, Abelardo. 1935.
Argentina.
Castillo, D. del. Mexico.
Castro Alves, Antônio de.
Brazil.
Castro, Consuelo de. 1946.
Brazil.
Castro, H. Alfredo. 1889.
Costa Rica.
Castro, Luiz Paiva de.
Brazil.
Centeno de Osma, Gabriel.
Peru.
Centeno Güell, Fernando.
1908. Costa Rica.
Cereceda, Verónica. Chile.
Césaire, Aimé. Martinique.
César Muniz, Lauro. Brazil.
Chalbaud, Román. 1931.
Venezuela.
Chaves, Mauro. Brazil.
Chaves Neto, João Ribeiro.
Brazil.
Chen, Ari. Brazil.
Chocrón, Isaac. 1933.
Venezuela.
Cid Pérez, José. Argentina.
Cisneros, José Antonio.
Mexico.
Coelho Júnior, Hélio Gomes.
Brazil.
Comorera, Juan.
Comunidad de San Miguelito.
Panamá.
Condé, Maryse.
Conteris, Hiber. Uruguay.
Cordero C., Gustavo.
Coronel Urtecho, José. 1906.
Nicaragua.
Corrêa, Viriato. Brazil.
Cortázar, Julio. 1914.
Argentina.
Cossa, Roberto M. 1934.
Argentina.
Costa, Odir Ramos da. Brazil.
Cruz, Casto Eugenio. Mexico.
Cruz, Sor Juana Inés de la.
1648. Mexico.
Cruz, Víctor Hugo.
Guatemala.
Cuadra, Fernando. Chile.
Cuadra, Pablo Antonio. 1912.
Nicaragua.
Cuartas, Joaquín. Cuba.

Cuchi Coll, Isabel. Puerto
Rico.
Cuéllar, José Tomás de.
1830. Mexico.
Curado, Ada. 1916. Brazil.
Cuzzani, Agustín. 1924.
Argentina.
Damel, Carlos S. Chile.
Dângelo, Jota. Brazil.
Darthés, Juan Fernando
Camilo. Chile.
Dávila V., Jorge E. Ecuador.
Debesa, Fernando. 1921.
Chile.
Defilippis Novoa, Francisco.
Deive, Carlos Esteban.
Dominican Republic.
Demichelli, Tulio. Argentina.
Denevi, Marco. 1922.
Argentina.
Desaloma, Roberto Daniel.
Argentina.
Devoy, Nené. Argentina.
Diament, Mario. Argentina.
Dias, Gonçalves. Brazil.
Díaz Díaz, Oswaldo.
Colombia.
Díaz, Francisco. El
Salvador.
Díaz González, O. Cuba.
Díaz, Gregor. 1933. Peru.
Díaz, Jorge. 1930.
Argentina.
Díaz Vargas, Henry.
Colombia.
Diego, Celia de. Argentina.
Discépolo, Armando. 1887.
Argentina.
Discépolo, Enrique Santos.
1901. Argentina.
Domingos, Anselmo. Brazil.
Domingos, José. Brazil.
Domínguez, Franklin. 1931.
Dominican Republic.
Dorr, Nicolás. 1947. Cuba.
Dragún, Osvaldo. 1929.
Argentina.
Dürst, Walter George.
Brazil.
Echevarría Loría, Arturo.
Costa Rica.
Eichelbaum, Samuel. 1894.
Argentina.
Elizalde, Fernando de.
Argentina.

Emery, Milton de Moraes.
    Brazil.
Endara, Ernesto. Panama.
Enríquez Gamón, Efraín.
    Paraguay.
Escobar, Carlos Henrique de.
    Brazil.
Espinosa Medrano, Juan de.
    1640. Peru.
Estevanell, Justo Esteban.
    Cuba.
Esteve, Patricio. Argentina.
Estorino, Abelardo. 1925.
    Cuba.
Fabian, Wanda. Brazil.
Farias Brasini, Mário. 1921.
    Brazil.
Felipe, Carlos. Cuba.
Fernandes, Millôr. 1923.
    Brazil.
Fernández de Lizardi, José
    Joaquín. 1776. Mexico.
Fernández, Francisco F.
    1842. Argentina.
Fernández Vilaros, F. Cuba.
Ferrari Amores, Alfonso.
    Argentina.
Ferrari, Juan Carlos. 1917.
    Argentina.
Ferreira, Helvécio. Brazil.
Ferrer, Rolando. 1925. Cuba.
Ferreti, Aurelio. 1907.
    Argentina.
Figueiredo, Guilherme de.
    1915. Brazil.
Filippis, Jorge. Argentina.
Filloy, Juan. 1894.
    Argentina.
Florit, Eugenio. 1903. Cuba.
França Júnior, Joaquim
    José da. Brazil.
Francovich, Guillermo. 1901.
    Bolivia.
Frank, Miguel.
Fuentes, Carlos. 1928.
    Mexico.
Galich, Manuel. 1912.
    Guatemala.
Galindo, Alejandro. Mexico.
Gallegos, Daniel. Costa Rica.
Gámbaro, Griselda. 1928.
    Argentina.
Gandara, Enrique.
    Argentina.

Gangá, C. Cuba.
Gann, Myra. Mexico.
García Guerra, Iván. 1938.
    Dominican Republic.
Garcia, Iván.
García Jaime, Luis. Ecuador.
García Márquez, Gabriel.
    1928. Colombia.
García Ponce, Juan. 1932.
    Mexico.
García Saldaña,
    Parménides.
García Velloso, Enrique.
    1880. Argentina.
Garibay, Ricardo. 1923.
    Mexico.
Garro, Elena. 1920. Mexico.
Gaviria, José Enrique.
    Colombia.
Gemba, Oraci. Brazil.
Gentile, Guillermo.
    Argentina.
Ghiano, Juan Carlos. 1920.
    Argentina.
Gil Gilbert, Enrique. 1912.
    Ecuador.
Gill Camargo, Roberto.
    Brazil.
Glissant, Edouard. Haiti.
Goldenberg, Jorge. Cuba.
Góes, Yara Ferraz de.
    Brazil.
Gomes, Alfredo Dias. 1914.
    Brazil.
Gomes, Roberto. Brazil.
Gómez de Avellaneda,
    Gertrudis. 1814. Cuba.
Gómez Masía, Román. 1903.
    Argentina.
Gondim Filho, Isaac. Brazil.
González Bocanegra,
    Francisco. Mexico.
González Caballero, Antonio.
    1931. Mexico.
González Cajiao, Fernando.
    Colombia.
González Castillo, José.
González Dávila, J. Mexico.
González de Cascorro, Raúl.
    Cuba.
González de Eslava, Fernán.
    1534. Mexico.
Gonzalez Delvalle,
    Alcibíades. Paraguay.

González González, Sergio.
Cuba.
González, Juan. 1924.
Venezuela.
Gorostiza, Carlos. 1920.
Argentina.
Gorostiza, Celestino. 1904.
Mexico.
Gorostiza, Manuel Eduardo de.
1789. Mexico.
Granada, Nicolás. 1840.
Argentina.
Gregorio, Jesús. Cuba.
Grisolli, Paulo Affonso.
Brasil.
Grupo Aleph. Chile.
Grupo La Candelaria.
Colombia.
Grupo Octubre. Argentina.
Grupo Ollantay. Ecuador.
Guarnieri, Gianfrancesco.
Brazil.
Guérin, Mona. Haiti.
Guerra, Ruy. Brazil.
Guerrero, Julio J. Peru.
Gullar, Ferreira. Brasil.

Gullar, José Ribamar
Ferreira. 1930. Brazil.
Gunther, Luiz Eduardo.
Brazil.
Gurrola, Juan José. Mexico.
Gutemberg, Luiz. Brazil.
Gutiérrez, Eduardo. 1853.
Argentina.
Gutiérrez, Ignacio. 1929.
Cuba.
Guzmán Améstica, Juan.
1931. Chile.
Halac, Ricardo. 1935.
Argentina.
Heiremans, Luis Alberto.
1928. Chile.
Helfgott, Sarina. Peru.
Henríquez, May.
Heredia, José María. 1803.
Cuba.
Herme, Juan Carlos.
Argentina.
Hernández, Luisa Josefina.
1928. Mexico.
Herrera, Ernesto. 1886.
Uruguay.
Herrera, Larry. Venezuela.

Hidalgo, Alberto. 1897. Peru.
Holanda, Nestor de. 1921.
Brazil.
Hollanda, Chico Buarque.
Brazil.
Ibargüengoitia, Jorge. 1928.
Mexico.
Icaza, Alberto.
Imbert, Julio. 1918.
Argentina.
Inclán, Federico S. 1910.
Mexico.
Jacintha, Maria. Brazil.
Jesús Martínez, Joé de.
Panama.
Jiménez Izquierdo, Joan.
Mexico.
Jockyman, Sérgio. 1930.
Brazil.
Jodorowsky, Alexandro.
Mexico.
Joffre, Sara. Peru.
Jordão, Yolanda. Brazil.
Jorge, Miguel. Brazil.
Júnior, França. Brazil.
Justo de Lara see Armas y
Cárdenas, José de.
Kosta, Leonardo. Ecuador.
Kraly, Néstor. Argentina.
Laferrère, Gregorio de.
1867. Argentina.
Lainez, Daniel. 1914.
Honduras.
Lanz, Joaquín. Mexico.
Larreta, Antonio. 1922.
Uruguay.
Lasser, Alejandro. 1916.
Venezuela.
Laura, Ida. Brazil.
Ledesma, Oscar. Mexico.
Legido, Juan Carlos. 1920.
Uruguay.
Leguizamón, Martiniano P.
1858. Argentina.
Lehmann, Marta. Argentina.
Lemaitre, Eduardo. Colombia.
Leñero, Vicente. 1933.
Mexico.
Leonardos, Stella see Lima,
Stella Leonardos da
Silva.
Lerner, Elisa. Venezuela.
Levi, Clóvis. Brazil.

Libre Teatro Libre (Group).
Argentina.
Lima, Edy. Brazil.
Lima, Stella Leonardos da
Silva. 1923. Brazil.
Lino Cayol, Roberto.
Argentina.
Lins, Osman. Brazil.
Lizardi, Fernández de.
Mexico.
Lizárraga, Andrés. 1919.
Argentina.
Llanos Aparicio, Luis.
Bolivia.
López Arellano, José.
Mexico.
López Pérez, Heriberto.
Colombia.
López, Willebaldo. Mexico.
Loredo, Rómulo. Cuba.
Lourenço, Pasqual. Brazil.
Luaces, Joaquín Lorenzo.
Cuba.
Luiz, Milton. Brazil.
Luna, J. Mexico.
Luna López, Estela. Peru.
Luna, Nelson. Brazil.
Macaya Lahmann, Enrique.
Costa Rica.
Macêdo, Joaquim Manoel de.
Brazil.
Machado de Assis, Joaquim
Maria. Brazil.
Machado, María Clara.
Brazil.
Macouba, Auguste. Martinique.
Magalhães, Gonçalves de.
Brazil.
Magalhães Júnior, Raymundo.
Brazil.
Magalhães, Paulo de. Brazil.
Magaña-Esquivel, Antonio.
1909. Mexico.
Magaña, Sergio. 1924.
Mexico.
Maggi, Carlos. 1922. Uruguay.
Maia, Arthur. Brazil.
Maia, Luiz. Brazil.
Maldonado Pérez, Guillermo.
Cuba.
Malfatti, Arnaldo. Argentina.
Mancuso, Delmar. Brazil.
Mantovani Abeche, Alfredo.
Brazil.

Maranhão Filho, Luiz.
Brazil.
Maranhão, José. Brazil.
Marcos de Burros, Plínio.
Brazil.
Marechal, Leopoldo. 1900.
Argentina.
María, Enrique de. 1870.
Argentina.
Marín, Gerard Paul. Puerto
Rico.
Marín, Luis. Ecuador.
Marinuzzi, Raul. Brazil.
Mármol, Jose. 1818.
Argentina.
Marques Andrade, Euclides.
Brazil.
Marqués, René. 1919. Puerto
Rico.
Martí, José. 1853. Cuba.
Martínez Arango, Gilberto.
Colombia.
Martínez, José de Jesús.
1929. Nicaragua.
Martínez Payva, Claudio.
1887. Argentina.
Martínez Queirolo, José.
1931. Ecuador.
Mauricio, Julio. 1919.
Argentina.
Medina, Roberto Nicolás.
Argentina.
Mejía, Medardo. Honduras.
Mellado, M. Cuba.
Mello, Zuleika. Brazil.
Melo, Fernando. Brazil.
Mendes, Alejandro Samuel.
Bolivia.
Méndez Ballester, Manuel.
1909. Puerto Rico.
Mendez Quiñones.
Mendive, Rafael Maria de.
Cuba.
Menén Desleal, Alvaro. El
Salvador.
Menéndez, Roberto Arturo.
1931. El Salvador.
Menezes, Constanza.
Argentina.
Menezes, Maria Wanderley.
Brazil.
Mertens, Federico. 1886.
Argentina.

Milanés, José Jacinto.
   1814. Cuba.
Mohana, João. 1925. Brazil.
Molleto, Enrique. 1922.
   Chile.
Mombrú, Maria. Argentina.
Monasterios, Rubén.
   Venezuela.
Monner Sans, José María.
   1896. Argentina.
Montaine, Eliseo. Argentina.
Montalvo, Juan. 1832.
   Ecuador.
Montaña, Antonio. 1932.
   Colombia.
Monteagudo, Bernardo.
   Bolivia.
Monteiro, José Maria.
   Brazil.
Monteiro, Marília Gama.
   Brazil.
Montes Huidobro, Matías.
   1931. Cuba.
Monti, Ricardo. Argentina.
Mora, Juan Miguel de. Mexico.
Moraes, Antônio Santos.
   Brazil.
Morales Alvarez, R. Cuba.
Morales, Jacobo. Puerto Rico.
Morales, José Ricardo.
   Chile.
Moreira, Fernando. Brazil.
Morete, María Luisa.
   Argentina.
Moreyra, Álvaro. 1888.
   Brazil.
Morris, Andrés. 1928.
   Spain/Honduras.
Mossi, Miguel Ángel.
Muello, Juan Carlos.
   Argentina.
Muniz, Lauro César. Brazil.
Nalé Roxlo, Conrado. 1898.
   Uruguay.
Naranjo, Carmen. Costa Rica.
Nari, Fortunato E. Argentina.
Navajas Cortés, Esteban.
   Cuba.
Navarro Carranza, Francisco.
   Mexico.
Negri, Nilton. Brazil.
Neruda, Pablo. 1904. Chile.
Neto, Coelho. Brazil.
Neves, João das. Brazil.

Niño, Jairo Anibal see
   Anibal Niño, Jairo.
Novión, Alberto.
Novo, Salvador. 1904. Mexico.
Novoa, Mario. 1939. Cuba.
Nunes, Carlos Alberto.
   Brazil.
Nunes, Cassiano. Brazil.
Nuñez, José Gabriel. 1937.
   Venezuela.
Nuñez, Nicolás. Mexico.
Oliva, Felipe. Cuba.
Oliveira, Domingos de.
   Brazil.
Oliveira, Pernambuco de.
   Brazil.
Oliveira, Valdemar de.
   Brazil.
Olmos, Carlos. Mexico.
Oporto, Walter. Argentina.
Orihuela, Roberto. Cuba.
Orozco Castro, Jorge. Costa
   Rica.
Ortega, Julio. 1942. Peru.
Orthof, Sylvia. Brazil.
Osoria, Luis Enrique. 1886.
   Colombia.
Ospina, Sebastián. Colombia.
Pacheco, Carlos Mauricio.
   1881. Argentina.
Pacheco, Tânia. Brazil.
Pagano, José León. 1875.
   Argentina.
Palant, Jorge. Argentina.
Palant, Pablo. 1914.
   Argentina.
Pallottini, Renata. Brazil.
Palomares, Francisco. Mexico.
Paola Levín, Jorge di.
   Argentina.
Paoli, Carlos de.
Pardo y Aliaga, Felipe. 1806.
   Peru.
Parra, Nicanor. 1914. Chile.
Parrado, Gloria. Cuba.
Pasos, Joaquín. 1915.
   Nicaragua.
Pavlovsky, Eduardo A.
   Argentina.
Payró, Roberto Jorge. 1867.
   Argentina.
Paz, Octavio. 1914. Mexico.
Pedroso, Bráulio. Brazil.
Pelayo, Félix M. Argentina.

Peña, Edilio. Venezuela.
Peón y Contreras, José.
  1843. Mexico.
Pequeño, P. N. Cuba.
Peregrina Corona, S. Mexico.
Pérez-Carmona, Juan. 1930.
  Argentina.
Pérez Luna, Edgardo. 1928.
  Peru.
Pérez Pardella, Agustín.
  Argentina.
Pérez Rey, Lupe. Costa Rica.
Petit de Murat, Ulises. 1905.
  Argentina.
Petraglia, Cláudio. Brazil.
Pfuhl, Oscar von. Brazil.
Philoctête, René. Haiti.
Pimentel, Altimar de Alencar.
  Brazil.
Pineda, José. Chile.
Piñera, Virgilio. 1912.
  Cuba.
Pinheiro, Jair. Brazil.
Pinto, Gilberto. 1930.
  Venezuela.
Pires, Meira. Brazil.
Plá, Josefina. 1909.
  Canarias/Paraguay
Ponferrada, Juan Oscar. 1908.
  Argentina.
Pongetti, Henrique. Brazil.
Pontes, Paulo. Brazil.
Porfírio, Pedro. Brazil.
Porto,, Oswaldo de. Brazil.
Portocarrero, Elena. Peru.
Prata, Mário. 1946. Brazil.
Qorpo-Santo, José Joaquim de
  Campos Leão. Brazil.
Queiroz, Rachel de. Brazil.
Queiroz Telles, Carlos de.
  Brazil.
Quintana, J. M. de. Cuba.
Quintero, Héctor. Cuba.
Quintero, Lucía. Puerto
  Rico/Venezuela.
Rabinovich, José. Argentina.
Radde, Ronald. Brazil.
Ramírez Farías, Carlos.
  Venezuela.
Ramírez Heredia, Rafael.
  Mexico.
Rangel, Flávio. Brazil.
Razo, Mario del. Mexico.
Rebolledo, Efrén. 1877.
  Mexico.

Rechani Agrait, Luis. Puerto
  Rico.
Reguera Saumell, Manuel.
  1928. Cuba.
Rengifo, César. 1915.
  Venezuela.
Requena, María Asunción.
  1918. Chile.
Retes, Ignacio. 1918. Mexico.
Reuben, William. Costa Rica.
Revueltas, José. 1914.
  Mexico.
Rey, Marcos. Brazil.
Reyes, Carlos José. 1941.
  Colombia.
Reyes de la Maza, Luis.
Reyes García, Ismael. Puerto
  Rico.
Reyes Ortiz, Félix. Bolivia.
Reyes Palacios, F. Mexico.
Rial, José Antonio.
  Venezuela.
Ribeyro, Julio Ramón. 1929.
  Peru.
Rio, João da. Brazil.
Rio, Marcela del. Mexico.
Rivarola Matto, José María.
Rivas, Ana. Argentina.
Rivera Saavedra, Juan. Peru.
Robles, J. Humberto. 1921.
  Mexico.
Rocha, Aurimar. Brazil.
Rocha Filho, Ruben. Brazil.
Rocha Miranda, Edgard de.
  Brazil.
Rodrigues, Elza Corrêa.
  Brazil.
Rodrigues, José Maria.
  Brazil.
Rodrigues, Nelson. 1912.
  Brazil.
Rodríguez Castelo, Hernán.
  Ecuador.
Rodríguez Galván, Ignacio.
  1816. Mexico.
Rodríguez, Jorge Mario.
  Argentina.
Rodriguez Muños, Alberto.
  Argentina.
Rodríguez Solís, Eduardo.
  Mexico.
Rodríguez Suárez, Roberto.
  Puerto Rico.
Roepke, Gabriela. Chile.
Roitman, Bernardo. Argentina.
Rojo, Gabriel. Chile.

Román, Sergio. Ecuador.
Römer, Raúl.
Romero, Mariela. Venezuela.
Rosario, Agustín del.
Rosencof, Mauricio. 1934.
  Uruguay.
Rovinski, Samuel. 1932. Costa
  Rica.
Rozenmacher, Germán N.
  Argentina.
Rozsa, Jorge. 1923.
  Hungary/Bolivia.
Rubens, Erwin Félix.
  Argentina.
Ruiz Cana y Sáenz Galiano,
  Francisco Antonio. 1732.
  Peru.
Sáenz, Dalmiro. 1926.
  Argentina.
Salas, M. Cuba.
Salazar Bondy, Sebastián.
  1924. Peru.
Salazar Támariz, Hugo. 1930.
  Ecuador.
Salcedo, José Manuel. Chile.
Saldarriaga Sanín, Rodrigo.
  Mexico.
Salinas, Pablo. Mexico.
Salmón, Raúl. Bolivia.
Sampaio, José da Silveira.
  Brazil.
San Felíx, Alvaro. Ecuador.
Sánchez, Florencio. 1875.
  Uruguay.
Sánchez, Luis Rafael. 1936.
  Puerto Rico.
Sánchez Mayans, Fernando.
  Mexico.
Sándor, Malena. Argentina.
Sanromán, Miguel Angel.
  Mexico.
Santana Salas, Rodolfo. 1944.
  Venezuela.
Santos, Benjamin. Brazil.
Santos, Vital. Brazil.
Schinca, Milton. 1926.
  Uruguay.
Schön, Elizabeth. Venezuela.
Schwarz, Roberto. Brazil.
Scolni, Miguel. Argentina.
Segall, Maurício. Brazil.
Seguín, Carlos Alberto.
  Peru.
Segura, Manuel Ascensio.
  1805. Peru.

Sequeira, J. Antônio de.
  Brazil.
Serra, Silvano. Brazil.
Serrano Marínez, C. Mexico.
Serulle, Haffe. Dominican
  Republic.
Shand, William. Argentina.
Sharim Paz, Nissim. Chile.
Sieveking, Alejandro. 1934.
  Chile.
Silva, Eurico. Brazil.
Silva, Francisco Pereira da.
  Brazil.
Silva, Hélcio Pereira da.
  Brazil.
Silva, Jaime. Chile.
Silveira, Miroel. Brazil.
Silvino, Paulo. Brazil.
Soberón Torchia, Edgar.
  Panama.
Sola Franco, Eduardo.
  Ecuador.
Solana, Rafael. 1915. Mexico.
Solari Swayne, Enrique.
Solórzano, Carlos. 1922.
  Guatemala.
Somigliani, Carlos.
  Argentina.
Soria, Ezequiel. Argentina.
Sotelo H., Aureo. Peru.
Souto, Alexandrino de.
  Brazil.
Souza, Jadir Vilela de.
  Brazil.
Souza, M. Brazil.
Speranza, Rolando. Uruguay.
St. Jean, Serge. Haiti.
Steiner, Rolando. 1936.
  Nicaragua.
Storni, Alfonsina. 1892.
  Argentina.
Strassberg, Sara. Argentina.
Suárez Figueroa, Sergio.
  Bolivia.
Suarez Radillo, Carlos
  Miguel.
Suassuna, Ariano. 1927.
  Brazil.
Taibo, Francisco Ignacio.
  Mexico.
Talesnik, Ricardo. Argentina.
Tálice, Roberto A. 1902.
  Argentina.
Tamayo, J. Cuba.
Tapia y Rivera, Alejandro.
  1827. Puerto Rico.

Tavares, Severino M. Brazil.
Telles, C. Q. Brazil.
Téllez, L. Mexico.
Tenorio, M. A. Mexico.
Thomas, José de. Argentina.
Tobar García, Francisco.
   1928. Ecuador.
Tojeiro, Gatão. Brazil.
Torcello de Devincenzi,
   Francisca see Devoy,
   Nené
Torres, Fielden. Ecuador.
Torres Molina, Susana.
   Argentina.
Torres Pita, Carlos. Cuba.
Torres, Victor. Cuba.
Torroella, Alfredo. Cuba.
Toscano, Carmen. Mexico.
Tourinho, Nazareno. Brazil.
Tovar, Juan. Mexico.
TPB. Colombia.
Trejo, Nemesio. 1862.
   Argentina.
Triana, José. 1933. Cuba.
Trouillot, Henock. Haiti.
Trujillo, Manuel. 1925.
   Venezuela.
Uriz, Francisco.
Urondo, Francisco. 1930.
   Argentina.
Urquizo, Francisco L. 1891.
   Mexico.
Urquizo Huici, Carlos
   Fernando. Bolivia.
Urruty, Esteban. Argentina.
Urueta, Margarita. 1918.
   Mexico.
Usigli, Rodolfo. 1905.
   Mexico.
Uslar Braun, Arturo.
   Venezuela.
Vacarezza, Alberto. 1896.
   Argentina.
Vadell, Jaime. Chile.
Valdés Vivó, Raúl. Cuba.
Valerio, J. F. Cuba.
Valle Filho, Esmerino Ribeiro
   do. Brazil.
Vallejo, César. 1892. Peru.
Valluzi, José. Brazil.
Vanegas Arroyo, Antonio.
   Mexico.
Varela, Cruz.
Veiga, Pedro. Brazil.
Velásquez, G. Mexico.

Veloz Maggiolo, Marcia. 1936.
   Dominican Republic.
Viana, O. Argentina.
Vianna Filho, Oduvaldo.
   Brazil. 1936.
Vianna, Oduvaldo. 1892.
   Brazil.
Vicente, José. Brazil.
Vieira, César. Brazil.
Vilalta, Maruxa. 1932.
   Spain/Mexico.
Villafañe, Javier. 1910.
   Argentina.
Villaurrutia, Xavier. 1903.
   Mexico.
Villegas, Oscar. Mexico.
Viñas, David. 1929.
   Argentina.
Vinos, Ricardo.
Viotti, Sérgio. Brazil.
Viteri, Eugenia. 1935.
   Ecuador.
Vlademir, José. Brazil.
Vodanović, Sergio. 1928.
   Chile.
Vulgarín, Agustín. Ecuador.
Wagner, Fernando. Mexico.
Walsh, Rodolfo. 1927.
   Argentina.
Wanderley, José. Brazil.
Wehbi, Timochenko. Brazil.
Williams, Paul. 1942.
   Venezuela.
Wolff, Egon. 1926. Chile.
Worm, Fernando. Brazil.
Ycaza, Alberto see Icaza,
   Alberto
Yglesias, Antonio. Costa
   Rica.
Zamacuco. Ecuador.
Zarlenga, Ethel Gladys.
   Argentina.
Zavala Cataño, Victor. Peru.

Author Index: Sample Entries

Garro, Elena.
    Arbol, El (Mexico : Rafael Peregrina Editor, 1967;
        30/3878)
    Felipe Angeles. In per. CO, 8, otoño 1967, p.1-35
        (32/4432a)
    Perros, Los. In anthol. 30/3857

Explanation.

    The first, "El Arbol", is a separately published play, a
stand-alone work. An annotation can be found in the Handbook of Latin
American Studies, volume 30, under entry number 3878.

    The second, "Felipe Ángeles", was published in the periodical
Coatl (code CO) for October 1967, on pages 1-35. An annotation can be
found in the Handbook of Latin American Studies, volume 32, under
entry number 4432a.

    The third, "Los Perros", was included in an anthology. The
complete bibliographic description of the anthology can be found under
code number 30/3857 in the List of Collections and Anthologies (page
114). A brief note about the play can be found in the Handbook of
Latin American Studies, volume 30, under entry number 3857.

Acero, Julio.
Hombre que perdió su sombra, El. In coll. 34/3356

Acevedo Hernández, Antonio.
Chañarcillo. (Santiago : Ed. Ercilla, 1970; 36/6750)

Acosta, Ricardo.
Agua linda. In anthol. 34/4048

Adellach, Alberto.
Chau Papá. In coll. 40/7236; also in anthol.
40/7314
Esa canción. In coll. 40/7236
Homo dramaticus. In coll. 40/7236

Adoum, Jorge Enrique.
Sol bajo la pata de los caballos, El. In per. CDLA/CO,
14, sept./dic. 1972, p.43-85.(36/6751)

Agüero Gómez, Gilberto.
Ciclón sobre los barcos de papel. (Maracaibo :
Universidad del Zulia, Facultad de Humanidades,
1967; 30/3844)
Identificación, La. In per. RT, 1:1, nov. 1967,
p.8-13. (32/4395)

Aguiar, Cláudio.
Flor destruida (São Paulo : Editora do Escritor, 1976;
40/7603)

Aguilera Malta, Demetrio.
Dientes blancos. In coll. 34/3993; also in anthol.
38/7202
España leal. In coll. 34/3993
Fantoche. In coll. 34/3993
Honorarios. In coll. 34/3993; also in anthol.
38/7202
Infierno negro. (Xalapa : Universidad Veracruzana, 1967;
30/3845); also in coll. 34/3993; also in anthol.
34/4046
Lázaro. In coll. 34/3993
Muerte, S. A. In coll. 34/3993
No bastan los Átomos. In coll. 34/3993
Tigre, El. In coll. 34/3993; also in anthol 00/7

Aguirre, Isidora.
    Carolina. In anthol. 30/3931a
    Los que van quedando en el camino. (Santiago,
        1970;34/3994); also in per. CDLA/CO, 3:8,
        julio/sept.1968, p.61-98. (32/4396)
    Papeleros, Los. In anthol. 34/4046; also in per.
        EC/M, 2:1,1964, p.57-93 (30/3846)
    Pérgola de las flores (radio adaptation). In anthol.
        38/7291

Aguirre, Yolanda.
    Muñeca negra, La. (La Habana : Biblioteca de Teatro
        Infantil, 1967; 30/3847)

Alban Gomez, Ernesto.
    Jeuves. In anthol. 00/10

Agustín, José.
    Atardeceres privilegiados de la prepa seis, Los. In
        anthol. 38/7161
    Círculo vicioso. (Mexico : Ed. Joaquín Mortiz, 1974;
        38/7150)

Alberto, Raimundo.
    Mansos da terra, Os. In per. RTB, 406, jan. 1975
        (40/7642)

Alegría, Alonso.
    Cruce sobre el Niágara, El. (La Habana : Casa de las
        Americas, 1969; 32/4396a)

Aliber, Alicia and Aliber, Bernardo.
    Mis abuelos campesinos. (Buenos Aires : Ediciones del
        Carro de Tespis, 1974; 42/5942)

Aliber, Bernardo see under Aliber, Alicia.

Almeida, Abilio Pereira de.
    Santa Marta Fabril sociedade anõnima   (Rio : Ministério
        da Educação e Cultura, Serviço Nacional de
        Teatro, 1973; 40/7604)

Almeida, Lyad de and Maia, Luiz.
    Cigarra e a Formiga, A. In per. RTB, num. 395, s/o '73
        (40/7642)

Almeida, Manuel Antônio de.
    Memórias de um sargento de milícias. (São Paulo :
        Editôra Brasiliense, 1965; 32/4860)

Alurista.
    Dawn. In anthol. 00/11

Alvarado, Manuel Luis.
    A cada cual su caos. In per. TALIA, 11:37, suplemento
        1970 (36/6752)

Alvarado, Rafael.
    De 7, 15 a 8 la entrada es por el aro, in per. RT, 1:2,
        dic. 1967/feb 1968, p.32-24 (32/4397)

Alves, Edgard G.
    Mulher zero quilômetro.   In per. RTB, num. 349, j/f '66

Amado, João Jorge.
    Oncilda e zé buscapé. In per. RTB, num. 416, m/a '77
        (40/7642)
    Quati Papa-ôvo, O.   In per. RTB, num. 379, j/f '71

Amaral, M. A.
    Cemitério sem cruzes. In anthol. 42/6366

Amaya Amador, Ramón.
    Peste Negra, La. In anthol. 42/5120a

Anchieta, José de.
    Auto de S. Sebastião (exc.). In coll. 42/6350
    Auto de Santa Ursula. In coll. 42/6350
    Auto representado na festa de São Lourenço (Rio :
        Ministério da Educação e Cultura, Serviço
        Nacional de Teatro, 1973; 40/7605). Also in coll
        32/6350
    Dia da assunção em reritiba. In coll. 42/6350
    Diálogo do P. Pero Dias Mártir. In coll. 42/6350
    Na aldeia de Guaraparim. In coll. 42/6350
    Na festa do natal ou pregação universal. In coll.
        42/6350
    Na vila de Vitória ou auto de S. Maurício. In coll.
        42/6350
    Na visitação de Santa Isabel. In coll. 42/6350
    Recebimento do P. Bartolomeu Simões Pereira. In coll.
        42/6350
    Recebimento do P. Marçal Beliarte. In coll. 42/6350
    Recebimento do P. Marcos da Costa. In coll. 42/6350

Andrade, Jorge.
    Milagre na cela. (Rio : Paz e Terra, 1977; 42/6351)
    Rasto atrás. (São Paulo : Editôra Brasiliense, 1967;
        34/4247)
    Telescópio, O (Rio : Ministério da Educação e
        Cultura, Serviço Nacional de Teatro, 1973; 40/7606)
    Zebra, A. In anthol. 42/6366

Andrade, Oswald de.
    Homem e o cavalo, O. In anth. 38/7525
    Morta, A. (Rio : Ministério da Educação e Cultura,
        Serviço Nacional de Teatro, 1973; 38/7524). Also
        in anthol. 38/7525
    Rei da vela, O. (São Paulo : Difusão Européia do Livro,
        1967; 34/4248). Also in anthol. 38/7525

Andrade Rivera, Gustavo.
    Camino, El. In per. CBR/BCB, 10:10, oct. 1967, p.169-191
        (32/4398)
    Farsa de la ignorancia y la intolerancia. In coll.
        38/7151
    Hombre que vendía talento, El. In coll. 38/7151
    Historias para quitar el miedo (radio adaptation)   In
        anthol 38/7291
    Propio veredicto, El. In coll. 38/7151. Also in per.
        CBR/BCB, 10:3, 1967, p.646-654 (30/3848)
    Remington 22. In coll. 38/7151. Also in anthol. 00/4
        and 34/4047; also radio adaptation in anthol.
        38/7291

Andreu Iglesias, César.
    Inciso hache, El.   In anthol. 00/12

Aníbal Niño, Jairo.
    Monte calvo, El.   In anthol. 40/7238. Also in per.
        ET/T, 1, oct. 1969, p.27-48 (36/6753)

Ankerman, Guillermo, jt. auth. see under Ankerman, Jorge

Ankerman, Jorge and Ankerman, Guillermo.
    Cosas de Cuba, Las. In per. UCLV/I, 51, mayo/agosto
        1975 (40/7237)
    Segunda república reformada, La. In per. UCLV/I, 51,
        mayo/agosto 1975 (40/7237)
    Todo por el honor. In per. UCLV/I, 51, mayo/agosto 1975
        (40/7237)

Antonietto, Elena.
    Mea culpa   (Buenos Aires : Talía; 40/7239)

Arango, Alfredo, jt. auth. see under Soberon Torchia, Edgar.

Arango, Gonzalo.
    Consagración de la nada, La. In coll. 32/4399
    Ratones van al infierno. In coll. 32/4399

Aranha, José Pereira da Graça.
    Malazarte   (Rio : Ministério da Educação e Cultura,
        Serviço Nacional de Teatro, 1973; 40/7607)

Araújo, Alcione.
    Há vagas para moças de fino trato.   In per.RTB, num.
        417, m/j '77 (40/7642)

Araújo, Nelson Correia de.
    1798, a conspiração dos alfaiates. In coll. 42/6352
    Discurso sobre o exílio na penha. In coll. 42/6352
    Grande escândalo e o paraiso de Agostinho da Piedade, O.
        In coll. 42/6352
    Joana Angélica. In coll. 42/6352
    Vinhetas de guerra holandesa. In coll. 42/6352

Arauz, Alvaro.
    Entre Medina y Ocampo. <u>In</u> anthol. 30/3857

Arce, Manuel José.
    Compermiso. <u>In</u> 36/6754
    De compras. <u>In</u> coll. 36/6754
    Delito, condena y ejecución de una gallina. <u>In</u> coll.
        36/6754
    Viva Sandino! : Pt. 1, Sandino debe nacer. <u>In</u> per. A,
        12, mayo/junio 1975, p.25-61 (38/7152)

Ardiles Gray, Julio.
    Arroz con leche... me quiero casar. <u>In</u> coll. 34/3997
    Gulliver. <u>In</u> coll. 34/3997
    Última cena, La. <u>In</u> coll. 34/3997
    Visita de novios. <u>In</u> coll. 34/3997

Arellano Guerra, Fausto E.
    Creación, La. <u>In</u> anthol. 00/10

Arevalo Martinez, Rafael.
    Duques de Endor, Los. <u>In</u> anthol. 00/13

Argüelles, Hugo.
    Cuervos están de luto, Los. <u>In</u> coll. 38/7153
    Tejedor de milagros, El. <u>In</u> coll. 38/7153
    Ronda de la hechizada, La. <u>In</u> anthol. 34/4023

Arinos, Afonso.
    Contratador dos diamantes, O (Rio : Ministério da
        Educação e Cultura, Serviço Nacional de Teatro,
        1973; 40/7608)

Arlt, Roberto.
    Africa.. <u>In</u> coll. 36/6755
    Desierto entra la ciudad, El. <u>In</u> coll. 36/6755
    Fabricante de fantasmas, El. <u>In</u> coll. 36/6755
    Fiesta del hierro, La. <u>In</u> coll. 36/6755
    Isla desierta, La. <u>In</u> coll. 30/3848a and 36/6755,
        <u>also in</u> anthol. 38/7183
    Prueba de amor. <u>In</u> coll. 36/6755
    Saverio el cruel. <u>In</u> coll. 30/3848a and 36/6755
    Trescientos millones. <u>In</u> coll. 36/6755

Armas y Cárdenas, José de.
    Triunfadores, Los. <u>In</u> anthol. 42/6010

Armijo, Roberto.
    Jugando a la gallina ciega. (San Salvador : Ministerio
        de Educación, Dirección General de Cultura,
        Dirección de Publicaciones, 1970; 34/3998)

Arreola, Juan José.
    Tercera llamada, tercera!, O empezamos sin Usted. <u>In</u>
        coll. 34/3366; <u>also in</u> anthol. 36/6806

Arriví, Francisco.
        Bolero y plena. In coll. 34/3999
        Club de solteros. In coll. 32/4400
        Coctel de Don Nadie. In anthol. 34/4040 and 36/6795
        Cuento de hadas, Un. In anthol. 34/4047
        María Soledad. In coll. 32/4400
        Sirena. In coll. 34/3999
        Una sombra menos see under new title María Soledad
        Vejigantes. In coll. 32/4400 and 34/3999; also in
                anthol. 32/4485

Arrufat, Antón.
        Caso se investiga, El. In anthol. 30/3886
        Repetición, La. In anthol. 00/7 and 34/4046
        Siete contra Tebas, Los. (La Habana : Ediciones Unión,
                1968; 32/4401)

Artiles, Freddy.
        Adriana en dos tiempos. (La Habana : Unión de Escritores
                y Artistas de Cuba, 1972; 36/6756)

Assaf, Jesús.
        Cuento de los dos jorobados. In anthol. 38/7162
        Estoy enamorado de tu hermana. In anthol. 34/3996 and
                38/7161

Assunção, Leilah.
        Da fala ao grito. (São Paulo : Edições Simbolo, 1977;
                42/6353)
        Sobrevividos. In anthol. 42/6366

Asturias, Miguel Angel.
        Audiencia de los confines, La. In coll. 00/14
        Chantaje. In coll. 00/14
        Dique Seco. In coll. 00/14
        Soluna. In coll. 00/14; also in anthol. 00/14; radio
                adaptation in anthol. 38/7291

Athayde, Roberto Austrogésilo de.
        Apareceu a Margarida. (Brasília : Editôra Brasília,
                1973; 38/7526; in French as Madame Marguerite
                in AVANT, n. 561, avr. '75

Aviles Blonda, Máximo.
        Otra estrella en el cielo, La. In coll. 32/4402
        Pirámide 179. In coll. 32/4402
        Yo, Bertolt Brecht. In coll. 32/4402

Ayala, Walmir.
        Chico Rei. In coll. 32/4861; also in per. RTB,
                num. 428, m/a '79 (40/7642)
        Nosso filho vai ser mãe. In coll. 32/4862
        Pobreza envergonhada, A. In anthol. 42/6381
        Quem matou Caim? In coll. 32/4862
        Salamanco do Jarau, A. In coll. 32/4861

Azar, Héctor.
 Alfarero, El. <u>In</u> coll. 40/7240
 Appassionata, La. <u>In</u> coll. 40/7240; <u>also in</u> anthol.
  34/4023
 Cabeza de Apolo, La. <u>In</u> coll. 38/7154
 Cantata de los emigrantes, La. <u>In</u> coll. 38/7154
 Copa de plata, La. <u>In</u> coll. 38/7154
 Corrido de Pablo Damián. <u>In</u> coll. 40/7240; <u>also in</u>
  anthol. 30/3857
 Doña Belarda de Francia. <u>In</u> coll. 7154
 Ensalada de pollos (adaptation) <u>In</u> anthol. 38/7187
 Higiene de los placeres y de los dolores. (México :
  Instituto Nacional de Bellas Artes, 1968; 32/4403)
  <u>Also in</u> anthol. 40/7283
 Inmaculada. (México : Organización Editorial Novaro,
  1972; 36/6757) <u>Also in</u> anthol. 40/7286
 Milagro y su retablo, El. <u>In</u> coll. 40/7240
 Muros vacíos, Los. (México : Textos CADAC, 1978;
  42/5943)
 Olímpica. <u>In</u> anthol. 30/3889a
 Paz (adapted from Aristophanes) <u>In</u> anthol. 38/7187
 Periquillo Sarniento (adaptation) <u>In</u> anthol. 38/7203
 Premio de excelencia, El. <u>In</u> coll. 40/7240
 Seda mágica, La. <u>In</u> coll. 38/7154
 Vacas flacas, Las. <u>In</u> coll. 38/7154

Azevedo, Artur.
 Capital Federal, A. (Rio : Editôra Letras e Artes,
  1965; 32/4863)
 Teatro a vapor. (São Paulo : Editora Cultrix, 1977;
  42/6354)

Azevedo, Manuel Antônio Alvares de.
 Macário. (Rio : Ministério da Educação e Cultura,
  Serviço Nacional de Teatro, 1972; 38/7527)

Baccaro, Julio.
 Cuando nos vamos. <u>In</u> per. TALIA, 9/10:35, 1969
  (32/4404)

Badía, Nora.
 Mañana es una palabra. <u>In</u> anthol. 30/3886

Baez, Edmundo.
 Alfiler en los ojos, Un. <u>In</u> anthol. 36/6779

Balla, Andrés.
 Los que respondieron al fuego (Buenos Aires : Autores
  Argentinos Asociados, 1975; 40/7241)
 Niña que bailaba, La. <u>In</u> anthol. 30/3849

Ballesté, Enrique.
 Mínimo quiere saber. <u>In</u> anthol. 38/7161
 Vida y obra de Dalomismo. <u>In</u> anthol. 36/6780

Bandrich, Agustín.
    Réquiem para lecumberri. In anthol. 42/5990

Barreto, Paulo.
    Eva. In per. RTB, num. 359/360, s/d '67
    Que pena ser só ladrão. In per. RTB, num. 353, s/o '66

Barros Grez, Daniel.
    Cada oveja con su pareja. In coll. 40/7242
    Como en Santiago. In coll. 40/7242; also in anthol.
        38/7183
    Ensayo de la comedia. In coll. 40/7242
    Vividor, El. In coll. 40/7242

Basurto, Luis G.
    Cada qien su vida. In anthol. 34/4023

Bauer, Luisa; Carballido, Emilio; and Wagner, F.
    Lámparas del cielo y de la tierra, Las. In anthol.
        38/7162

Belaval, Emilio S.
    Campo y el escritorio, El. In per. RRI, 3:3, Fall 1973,
        p.231-240 (38/7156)
    Circe; o, El amor. In anthol. 00/12
    Hay que decir la verdad. In per. PRAAC/B, 8:2/3,
        abril/sept. 1972, p.162-199 (40/7243)
    Puerto y la mar, El. In per. RRI, 3:3, Fall 1973,
        p.241-251 (38/7157)

Benavente P., David.
    Tengo ganas de dejarme barba. In per. EC/M, 17, 1968,
        p.97-152 (34/4000)

Benavente P., David, jt. auth. see under Vadell, Jaime.

Bender, Ivo.
    Auto do pastorzinho e seu rebanho. In coll. 40/7609
    Aventuras do super-espantalho contra o Dr. Corvo, As.
        In coll. 40/7609
    Cartas marcadas ou os assassinos, As. In coll. 40/7609
    Estrelinha cadente, A. In coll. 40/7609
    Macaco e a velha, O. In coll. 40/7609
    Quem roubou meu Anabela? In coll. 40/7609
    Queridíssimo canalha. In anthol. 42/6355
    Sexta feira das paixões. In anthol. 42/6355

Benedetti, Mario.
    Ida y vuelta. In coll. 32/4405
    Pedro y el capitán (México : Editorial Nueva Imagen,
        1979; 42/5944)
    Reportaje, El. In coll. 32/4405

Beneke, Walter.
    Funeral home. In coll. 40/7244
    Paraíso de los imprudentes, El. In coll. 40/7244

Benítez Pereira, Ovidio.
    Como la voz de muchas aguas (Asunción : Radio Charitas,
        1965; 30/3850)

Berrutti, Alejandro.
    Cuidado con los bonitas. In anthol. 42/5953
    Tres personnajes a la pesca de un autor. In anthol.
        00/1

Bethencourt, João.
    Como matar um playboy. In per. RTB, num. 372, n/d
        '69
    Crime roubado, O. In per. RTB, num. 403, j/f '75
        (40/7642)
    Frank Sinatra 4815. In per. RTB, num. 383, s/o '71
    Ilha de circe, A (Mister Sexo) (São Paulo : Editôra
        Brasiliense, 1966; 32/4864)

Betti, Atilio.
    Fundación del desengaño. In anthol. 38/7171

Bezerra Filho, José.
    Canudos (publisher not determined; 40/7610)

Bioy Casares, Adolfo.
    Siete soladores. In per. SUR, 314, julio/oct. 1968,
        p.21-35 (36/6758)

Bivar, Antônio.
    Abre a janela e deixa entrar o ar puro e o sol de
        manhã. In per RTB, num. 367, j/f '69
    Alzira Power. In per. RTB, num. 401, s/o '74 (40/7642)
    Cordélia Brasil. In per. RTB, num. 413, s/o '76
        (40/7642)
    Quarteto. In per. RTB. num. 426, n/d '78 (40/7642)

Blanco, Jorge.
    Dúo. In per. MN, 20, feb. '68, p.55-71 (30/3850a)

Bloch, Jonas, and Dângelo, Jota.
    Oh! Oh! Oh! (Minas Gerais : Editôra Itatiaia, 1968;
        36/7144)

Bloch, Pedro.
    Amor a oito mãos. In per. RTB, num. 344, m/a '65
    Contrato azul, O. In per. RTB, num. 384, n/d '71
        (38/7565)
    Dona Xepa (Petrópolis : Editôra Vozes, 1969; 34/4249;
        also Rio : Edições Nosso Tempo, 1977; 42/6356)
    Esta noite choveu prata. In coll. 30/4200
    Inimigos não mandam flôres, Os. In coll. 30/4200;
        also in per RTB, num. 374, m/a '70
    Karla, valeu a pena? In per. RTB, num. 414, n/d '76
        (40/7642)
    LSD. In per. RTB, num. 384, n/d '71 (38/7565)
    Mãos de Eurídice, As. In coll. 30/4200

Bloch, Pedro, cont'd.
    Morre um gato na China   (Petrópolis : Editôra Vozes,
        1969; 38/7528); also in per. RTB, num. 354, n/d
        '66
    Pais abstratos, Os   (Petrópolis : Editôra Vozes, 1965;
        36/7145); also in per RTB, num. 368, m/a '69
    Roleta Paulista.   In per. RTB, num. 335, s/o '63
    Soraia pôsto dois.   In per RTB, num. 339, m/j '64
    Sorriso de pedra, O.   In coll. 30/4200

Boal, Augusto.
    Gran acuerdo internacional del Tío Patilludo, El
        (transl. from Portuguese).   In coll 40/7611
    Revolución en América del Sur (transl. from
        Portuguese).   In coll. 40/7611
    Torquemada.   In anthol. 36/6801; also transl. from
        Portuguese in coll. 40/7611

Bocanegra, Matías de.
    Comedia de San Francisco de Borja.   In anthol. 42/5122

Bolón, Hugo.
    Water 2000   (Montevideo : Círculo Editorial, 1966;
        30/3851)

Bonnin Armstrong, Ana Inés.
    Difícil esperanza, La.   In anthol. 30/3933

Booi, Hubert.
    Golgotha.   In per. AC, 5:4, 1967, p.7-21 (30/3852)

Borba Filho, Hermilo.
    Donzela Joana, A   (Petrópolis : Editôra Vozes, 1966;
        32/4865)
    Sobrados e mocambos   (Rio : Civilização Brasileira,
        1972; 40/7612)

Borges, Durval.
    Bossa nova.   In coll. 38/7529
    Camélia branca.   In coll 38/7529
    Castigo.   In coll. 38/7529
    Justiça.   In coll. 38/7529
    Terra sem dono.   In coll. 38/7529

Borges, José Carlos Cavalcânti.
    Casa grande & senzala   (Rio : Ministério da Educação e
        Cultura, Serviço Nacional de Teatro, 1970; 38/7530)
    Flor e o fruto, A.   In per. RTB, num. 385, j/f '72
    Mão de môça, pé de verso   (Recife : Imprensa
        Universitária, 1965; 30/4201)
    Tempestade em fígua benta   (Recife : Imprensa
        Universitária, 1964; 30/4202)

Botelho de Oliveira, Manuel.
    Hay amigo para amigo   (Rio : Ministério da Educação e
        Cultura, Serviço Nacional de Teatro, 1973; 40/7613)

Botelho Gosálvez, Rául.
    Lanza capitana, La   (La Paz : Biblioteca Paceña, 1967;
        30/3853)

Braga, J. Alberto.
    Misterioso caso do queijo desaparecido, O. <u>In</u> per.
        RTB, num. 394, j/a '73 (40/7642)

Brasini, Mário.
    Guerra mais ou menos santa, A   (São Paulo : Editôra
        Brasiliense, 1965; 34/4250)

Brene, José R.
    Demonios de remedios, Los. <u>In</u> coll. 30/3855
    Fiebre negra, La. <u>In</u> coll. 30/3855
    Fray Sabino   (La Habana : Unión de Escritores y
        Artistas, 1971; 36/6759)
    Gallo de San Isidro, El   (La Habana : Ediciones
        Revolución, 1964; 30/3854)
    Ingenioso criollo, El. <u>In</u> coll. 30/3855

Bressan, Lindor, and others.
    Asesinato de X, El. <u>In</u> anthol. 36/6801

Britto García, Luis.
    Así es la Cosa. <u>In</u> coll. 40/7246
    Gula. <u>In</u> anthol. 42/6013
    Suena el teléfono. <u>In</u> coll. 40/7245
    Tirano Aguirre o la conquista de El Dorado, El. <u>In</u>
        coll. 40/7245
    Venezuela tuya. <u>In</u> coll. 40/7246

Buenaventura, Enrique.
    A la diestra de Dios Padre. <u>In</u> coll. 42/5945; in
        English as In the right hand of God the Father <u>in</u>
        anthol. 00/8
    Denuncia, La. <u>In</u> per. PRIA, 163/164, dic. 1973/ enero
        1974, p.40-58 (38/7158)
    Menú, El. <u>In</u> coll. 42/5945; <u>also in</u> anthol.
        34/4046; <u>also in</u> per. CDLA/CO, 3:10, dic. 1968,
        p.12-44 (34/4001)
    Orgía, La. <u>In</u> coll. 42/5945; in English as The Orgy
        <u>in</u> anthol. 00/5
    Papeles del Infierno, Los. <u>In</u> coll. 42/5945; in an
        English excerpt as The Twisted state <u>in</u> per. TDR,
        vol. 14, n. 2, Winter '70
    Soldados. <u>In</u> coll. 42/5945

Bustillo Oro, Juan.
    Mi hijo el Mexicano   (México : Editorial Enigma, 1966;
        30/3856)
    San Miguel de las Espinas. <u>In</u> anthol. 34/4023

Buttaro, Enrique.
    Distraídos, los; o la torta de la novia. <u>In</u> anthol.
        00/1 and 42/5953

Cabrera y Bosch, R.
    Arriba con el himno! In anthol. 40/7280
    Del parque a la lucocina. In anthol. 40/7280

Cabrera y Quintero, Cayetano Javier de.
    Acción cómico-alegórica. In coll. 42/5114a
    Coloquio al nacimiento de Nuestro Señor. In coll.
        42/5114a
    Coloquio al sorpedate de Nuestra Señora. In coll.
        42/5114a
    Empeños de la casa de la sabiduría. In coll.
        42/5114a
    Iris de Salamanca, El. In coll. 42/5114a
    Loa a Nuestra Señora del Rosario. In coll. 42/5114a
    Loa al nacimiento de Nuestro Señor. In coll. 42/5114a
    Loa en aplauso al reverendísimo padre fray Josef Pérez.
        In coll. 42/5114a
    Loa en celebridad de pascuas. In coll. 42/5114a
    Loa para la comedia del escondido y la tapada. In
        coll. 42/5114a
    Panegírico aplauso. In coll. 42/5114a
    Representación panegírica. In coll. 42/5114a
    Sainete y fin de fiesta. In coll. 42/5114a

Cabrujas, José Ignacio.
    Fiésole. In anthol. 34/4048
    Soberbia. In anthol. 42/6013

Caldas, Erasmo Catauli.
    Berço de ouro, O (Rio : Ministério da Educação e
        Cultura, Serviço Nacional de Teatro, 1969; 38/7531)
    Corgo do vau (Rio : Editôra Letras e Artes, 1965;
        32/4866)

Calderón, Manuel A.
    Diez años en Buenos Aires, Diciembre 1946-Junio 16 de
        1955 (Buenos Aires : Ediciones del Carro de Tespis,
        1967; 32/4406)

Calizaya Velásquez, Zenobio.
    Dad al César lo que es del César y a Dios lo que es de
        Dios. In anthol. 42/5949

Callado, Antônio.
    Forró no engenho cananéia (Rio : Editôra
        Civilização Brasileira, 1964; 32/4867)

Calvet, Aldo.
    Casa de Ninguém. In coll. 36/7146
    Dr. Judas. In coll. 36/7146
    Exhaustação. In coll. 36/7146
    Hortênsias, As. In per. RTB, num. 428, m/a '79
        (40/7642)
    Trompette. In coll. 36/7146

Calveyra, Arnaldo.
    Latin American trip   (Caracas : Monte Avila Editores,
        1978; 42/5946)

Câmara, Isabel.
    Moças: o beijo final, As. In per. RTB, num. 395, s/o
        '73 (40/7642)

Camargo, Joracy.
    Anastácio. In per. RTB, num. 392, m/a '73 (40/7642)
    Corpo de luz, Um. In coll. 40/7614
    Deus lhe pague. In coll. 40/7614
    Figueira do inferno. In coll. 40/7614
    Juizo final. In per RTB, num. 348, n/d '65
    Mocinha. In per. RTB, num. 338, m/a '64

Campos, Geir.
    Castro Alves ou O canto da esperança (Rio : Leitura,
        1972; 40/7615)
    Sementes da independência, As (Rio : Ministério da
        Educação e Cultura, Serviço Nacional de Teatro,
        1972; 38/7532)

Cañas, Alberto F.
    Algo más que dos sueños. In coll. 40/7247; also in
        anthol. 34/4047 and 40/7277; radio adaptation in
        anthol. 38/7291
    Bruja en el rio, Una (San José : Editorial Costa Rica,
        1978; 42/5947)
    Eficaz plan para resolver la desnutición infantil, y de
        paso los problemas fiscales. In coll. 40/7247
    En agosto hizo dos años (San José : Editorial Costa
        Rica, 1968; 32/4407). Also in coll. 40/7247
    Héroe, El. In coll. 40/7247; also in anthol. 36/6790
    Luto robado, El. In coll. 40/7247
    Segua, La. In coll. 40/7247

Cantón, Wilberto.
    Juego sagrado, El. In anthol. 00/7 and 30/3857
    Malditos. In coll. 36/6760
    Nosotros somos Dios. In English as We are God in per.
        DRAMA, vol. 10, n. 3, Spring '72
    Pecado mortal. In coll. 36/6760

Carballido, Emilio.
    Acapulco, los lunes (Monterrey : Ediciones Sierra
        Madre, 1969; 32/4408). Also in coll. 42/5948
    Antes cruzaban ríos. In per. RBA, 13:14, marzo/abril
        1967, p.4-7 (32/4408)
    Censo, El. In anthol. 00/7 and 30/3857
    Delicioso domingo. In per. S, 2, feb 1972, p.15-25
        (38/7160)
    Día que se soltaron los leones, El. In coll.
        40/7250; in English as Day they let the lions
        loose in anthol. 00/8

Carballido, Emilio, cont'd.
    Final de un idilio, El   (publisher not determined;
        36/6761)
    Fonda de las Siete Cabrillas, La. In per. RBA, 19,
        enero/feb. 1975, p.50-64 (40/7248)
    Guillermo y el Nahual. In anthol. 38/7162
    Hijos del Capitán Grant, Los. In anthol. 38/7187
    Lente maravillosa, La. In anthol.38/7167
    Medusa. In coll. 40/7250; also in anthol. 40/7283
    Noticias del día, Las (México : Col. Teatro de
        bolsillo, 1968; 30/3857a)
    Pastorela cinematográfica. In per. RBA, 24, nov./dic.
        1968, p.17-54 (36/6762)
    Pequeño día de ira. In coll. 42/5948
    Por si alguna vez soñamos. In per. C, 1:2, otoño
        1976, p.5-19 (40/7249)
    Relojero de Córdoba, El. In coll. 40/7250
    Rosalba y los llaveros. In coll. 40/7250
    Silencio, pollos pelones. In coll. 42/5948
    Te juro Juana, que tengo ganas... In per. UV/PH, 9:35,
        1965, p.487-530 (30/3858)
    Yo también hablo de la rosa (México : Instituto
        Nacional de Bellas Artes, 1966; 30/3859). Also in
        anthol. 00/2, 00/9, 34/4023, and 42/5986; in English
        as I too speak of the rose in per. DRAMA, vol. 8,
        n. 1

Carballido, Emilio, jt. auth. see under Bauer, Luisa.

Cárdenas, Raúl de.
    Palangana, La. In anthol. 30/3886

Cardoso, Lúcio.
    Escravo, O (Rio : Ministério da Educação e Cultura,
        Serviço Nacional de Teatro, 1973; 40/7616)

Cardozo, Joaquim.
    Antônio conselheiro. In coll. 38/7533
    Capataz de salema, O. In coll. 38/7533
    De um noite de festa (Rio : Livraria Agir Editora, 1971;
        40/7617)
    Marechal: boi de carro. In coll. 38/7533

Carella, Tulio.
    Don Basilio mal casado (Buenos Aires : Ediciones del
        Carro de Tespis, 1969; 34/4002)

Carlino, Carlos.
    Biunda, La (Buenos Aires : Ediciones del Carro de
        Tespis, 1969; 32/4409). Also in anthol. 38/7171

Carreño, Virginia, jt. auth. see under Menezes, Constanza.

Carrero, Jaime.
    Flag inside. In per. CDLA/CO, 25, julio/sept. 1975,
        p.20-48 (40/7251)

Carvalho, Antônio C.
     Obstétrica, ou o parto dos telefones   (Rio : Editôra
          Letras e Artes, 1965; 30/4203)

Carvalho, Carlos.
     Boneca Teresa, ou Canção de amor e morte de Gelsi e
          Valdinete. In anthol. 42/6355
     PT Saudações. In anthol. 42/6355

Carvalho, Hélio.
     Joãozinho me Maria. In per. RTB, num. 390, n/d '72
          (40/7642)

Carvalho, Hermínio Bello de.
     João Amor e Maria   (Rio : Gráfica Record Editôra,
          1966; 32/4868)

Casali, Renzo.
     Maximiliano diez años después.   In anthol. 40/7314

Castellanos, Rosario.
     Eterno femenino, El   (México : Fondo de Cultura
          Económica, 1975; 40/7252)
     Judith. In coll. 40/7253
     Poesía no eres tú (México : Fondo de Cultura
          Económica, 1972; 40/7253)
     Salomé. In coll. 40/7253

Castellanos de Ríos, Ada.
     Jugando a soñar. In anthol. 42/5949

Castillo, Abelardo.
     A partir de las siete. In coll. 32/4410
     Otro Judas, El. In coll. 32/4410
     Sobre las piedras de Jericó. In coll. 32/4410

Castillo, D. del.
     Desempleo, El. In anthol. 34/3996
     Riesgo, vidrio. In anthol. 38/7161

Castro Alves, Antônio de.
     Gonzaga ou a revolução de minas   (Rio : Ministério da
          Educação e Cultura, Serviço Nacional de Teatro,
          1972; 38/7535)

Castro, Consuelo de.
     A flôr da pele. In per. RTB, num. 382, j/a '71
     Caminho de volta. In per. RTB, num. 410, m/a '76
          (40/7642)
     Prova de fogo, A (São Paulo : Editora HUCITEC, 1977;
          42/6358)

Castro, H. Alfredo.
     Juego limpio. In anthol. 32/4459

Castro, Luiz Paiva de.
     Aquário, O (Rio : José Ívaro Editor, 1970; 38/7534)

Centeno de Osma, Gabriel.
     Pobre más rico, El. _In_ anthol. 38/6449

Centeno Güell, Fernando.
     Danzas de Job, Las (San José : Editorial Costa Rica,
          1977; 42/5950)

Cereceda, Verónica.
     Deportivo "El Guerrillero". _In_ per. UV/PH, 9:34, 1965,
          p.239-293 (30/3860)

Césaire, Aimé.
     Saison au Congo, Une (Paris : Editions du Seuil, 1966;
          also in English as Season in the Congo, New York :
          Grove, 1968 [Evergreen ed.]; also in German as Im
          Kongo, Berlin : Wagenbach, 1966)
     Tempête, Une (Paris, Editions du Seuil, 1969; 36/7173)
     Tragédie du roi Christophe, La (Paris : Présence
          Africaine, 1963; also in English as Tragedy of King
          Christophe, New York : Grove, 1970 [Evergreen ed.])

César Muniz, Lauro.
     Morte do imortal, A. _In_ per. RTB, num. 391, j/f '73
          (40/7642)

Chalbaud, Román.
     Angeles terribles, Los. _In_ anthol. 34/4048
     Ira. _In_ anthol. 42/6013
     Pinzas, Las. _In_ anthol. 34/4047; in English as Forceps
          _in_ anthol. 00/4
     Quema de Judas, La (Caracas : Univ. Central de
          Venezuela, Dirección de Cultura, 1965; 32/4411)

Chaves, Mauro.
     Virulêncio, O (São Paulo : Departamento de Artes e
          Ciências Humanas, Comissão de Teatro, 1979;
          42/6359)

Chaves Neto, João Ribeiro.
     Patética (Rio : Civilização Brasileire, 1978; 42/6360)

Chen, Ari.
     Excluso (Rio : Editôra Letras e Artes, 1965; 32/4869)

Chocrón, Isaac.
     Acompañante, El (Caracas : Monte Avila Editores, 1978;
          42/5951)
     Amoroso. _In_ coll. 32/4412
     Animales feroces. _In_ coll. 32/4412 and 42/5952
     Asia y el lejano oriente. _In_ coll. 42/5952
     Máxima felicidad, La (Caracas : Monte Avila, 1974;
          40/7254)

Chocrón, Isaac, cont'd.
　　OK　(Caracas : Monte Avila Editores, 1969; 34/4003)
　　Pereza. In anthol. 42/6013
　　Quinto infierno, El. In coll. 32/4412 and 42/5952
　　Revolución, La (Caracas : Editorial Tiempo Nuevo, 1972;
　　　　38/7163)
　　Tric Trac. In anthol. 34/4048

Cid Pérez, José.
　　Comedia de los muertos, La. In coll. 36/6763; in
　　　　English as Comedy of the dead in per FIRST, vol.
　　　　6, n. 1, Spring 67
　　Hombres de dos mundos. In coll. 36/6763
　　Y quiso más la vida. In coll. 36/6763

Cisneros, José Antonio.
　　Diego el mulato. In anthol. 36/6779

Coelho Júnior, Hélio Gomes, and Gunther, Luiz Eduardo.
　　Pássaro de louça (Curitiba, 1974; 42/6361)

Comorera, Juan, jt. author see under Gonzalez Castillo,
　　José

Comunidad de San Miguelito, Panamá.
　　Pasión de Cristo con Entraña Panameña, La [radio
　　　　adaptation] In anthol. 38/7291

Condé, Maryse.
　　Dieu nous l'a donné (Paris : Editions Pierre Jean
　　　　Oswald, 1972; 40/7779)

Conteris, Hiber.
　　Asesinato de Malcolm X, El (Montevideo : Ediciones
　　　　Mundo Nuevo, 1969; 34/4004). Also in per.
　　　　CDLA/CO, 2:5, oct./dic. 1967, p.27-68 (32/4413)

Cordero C., Gustavo.
　　Paralelo al sueño. In anthol. 00/10

Coronel Urtecho, José.
　　Petenera, La. In anthol. 40/7315
Coronel Urtecho, José, jt. auth. see under Pasos, J.

Corrêa, Viriato.
　　Juriti. In per RTB, num. 329, s/o '62
　　Maurício de Nassau. In per. RTB, num. 357, m/j '67

Cortázar, Julio.
　　Reyes, Los (Buenos Aires : Editorial Sudamericana,
　　　　1970; 32/4414)

Cossa, Roberto M.
　　Dias de Julián Bisbal, Los. In coll. 32/4415
　　Nata contra el libro, La. In anthol. 30/3861
　　Nuestro fin de semana. In coll. 32/4415 and 40/7271

Cossa, Roberto M.; Rozenmacher, Germán; Somigliana, Carlos;
    and Talesnik, Ricardo.
    Avión negro, El (Buenos Aires : Talía, 1970; 40/7257).
        Also in coll. 34/4051

Costa. Odir Ramos da.
    Sonho de uma noite de velório (Rio : Ministério da
        Educação e Cultura, Fundação Nacional de Arte,
        Serviço Nacioanl de Teatro, 1976; 42/6362)

Cruz, Casto Eugenio.
    Equipo de Salvamento. In anthol. 38/7162

Cruz, Sor Juana Inés de la.
    Loa para el auto sacramental de "El Divino Narciso".
        In anthol. 38/7183
    Sainete segundo. In anthol. 38/7183

Cruz, Victor Hugo.
    Dos y dos son cinco. In per. A, 4, enero/feb. 1974,
        p.26-38 (38/7164)

Cuadra, Fernando.
    Familia de Marta Mardones, La. In per. EC/M, 24,
        1977, p.103-166 (42/5954)
    Niña en la Palomera, La (Santiago : Ediciones
        Ercilla, 1970; 34/4005)

Cuadra, Pablo Antonio.
    Por los caminos van los campesinos. In anthol.
        40/7315

Cuartas, Joaquín.
    Llegó a la gloria la gente de los Santos Inocentes.
        In per. UV/PH, 10:39, 1966, p.459-501 (30/3862)

Cuchi Coll, Isabel.
    Familia de Justo Malgenio: Puertorriqueños en Nueva
        York, La (Madrid : Gráfica Internacional, 1974;
        42/5955)

Cuéllar, José Tomás de.
    Baile y cochino (adapted by Razo, Mario del, and
        Rodríguez, Azucena). In anthol. 38/7206

Curado, Ada.
    Sob o tormento da espera (Goiânia : Oriente, 1976;
        42/6363)
Cuzzani, Agustín.
    Libra de carne, Una. In coll. 38/7171
    Para que se cumplan las escrituras (Buenos Aires :
        Editorial Quetzal, 1965; 30/3863

Damel, Carlos S., jt. auth. see under Darthés, Juan
    Fernando Camilo.
Dângelo, Jota, jt. auth. see under Bloch, Jonas.

Darthés, Juan Fernando Camilo and Damel, Carlos S.
    Hermana Josefina, La. In English as Quack Doctor in
        anthol. 00/3

Dávila V., Jorge E.
    Con gusto a muerte. In per. CCE/NAR, 12:18, 1972,
        p.64-79 (36/6765)

Debesa, Fernando.
    Guardapelo, El. In per. EC/M, 4:1, 1965, p.57-66
        (30/3864)
    Guerrero de la paz, El. In per. EC/M, 18, verano 1969,
        p.113-164 (32/4417)
    Mama Rosa (Santiago : Editorial Universitaria, 1969;
        34/4006)
    Persona y perro. In anthol. 30/3931a
    Primera persona, singular. In per. UCCH/A, 33, oct.
        1963, p.4-22 (32/4418)

Defilippis Novoa, Francisco.
    Desventurados, Los. In anthol. 00/1
    Día sábado, El. In anthol. 00/1

Deive, Carlos Esteban.
    Hombre que nunca llegaba, El (Santo Domingo : Editora
        del Caribe, 1971; 34/4007)

Demichelli, Tulio, jt. auth. see under Petit de Murat, Ulises.

Denevi, Marco.
    Fracasados, Los. In coll. 34/4008
    Globo amarillo, Un. In coll. 34/4008
    Juramentos de una perjura, Los. In coll. 34/4008
    Segundo círculo, El. In coll. 34/4008

Desaloma, Roberto Daniel.
    Interrogatorio, El. In per. CDLA/CO, 13, mayo/agosto
        1972, p.24-57 (36/6766)

Devoy, Nené.
    Título para Laurina, Un (Buenos Aires : Escuela de Artes
        Gráficas, 1966; 30/3865)

Diament, Mario.
    Crónica de un secuestro (Buenos Aires : Editorial
        Talía, 1972; 36/6767)

Dias, Gonçalves.
    Leonor de Mendoça. In per. RTB, num. 340, j/a '64

Díaz Díaz, Oswaldo.
    Diana Valdés. In coll. 30/3870
    Fénix y la tórtola, El. In coll. 30/3870
    Gaitana, La. In coll. 30/3870
    Jaula de cristal, La. In coll. 30/3870
    Pretor, El (Bogotá, Editorial Kelly, 1967; 30/3869)

Díaz Díaz, Oswaldo, cont'd.
    Sopa del soldado, La. In coll. 30/3870

Díaz, Francisco.
    Muerte del general Francisco Morazán, La   (Tegucigalpa :
        Instituto Morazánico, 1976; 42/5956)

Díaz González, O.
    Caña y la remolacha, La. In anthol. 40/7280

Díaz, Gregor.
    Cercadores, Los. In anthol. 38/7204
    Cercados. In anthol. 38/7204
    Con los pies en el agua. In anthol. 38/7204
    Los del cuatro. In anthol. 34/4040

Díaz, Jorge.
    Cepillo de dientes, El. In coll. 32/4420 and 38/7166;
        also in anthol. 32/4424 and 42/5986
    Genesis fue mañana, El. In anthol. 00/7 and 30/3931a in
        English as Eve of the Execution, or Genesis was
        tomorrow in anthol. 00/5
    Introducción al elefante y otros zoologías. Excerpt in
        English as Man does not die by bread alone in per.
        T D R, vol. 14, n. 2, Winter '70
    Locutorio, El. In anthol. 42/5957
    Lugar donde mueren los mamíferos, El. In per. EC/M, 3:3,
        1965, p.107-142 (30/3866) in English as Place where the
        mammals die in anthol. 00/9
    Orgástula, La. In per. UK/LATR, 4:1, Fall 1970, p.79-85
        (34/4009)
    Pancarta, La, o Está estrictamente prohibido todo lo que no
        es obligatorio. In anthol. 38/7165
    Requiem por un girasol. In coll. 32/4420
    Topografía de un desnudo: esquema para una indagación
        inútil (Santiago : Editora Santiago, 1967; 30/3867)
    Velero en la botella, El. In coll. 38/7166; also in
        per. EC/M, 1:1, 1963, p.53-84 (30/3868) and PRIA, 69,
        1965, p.38-54 (32/4419)
    Víspera del degüello. In coll. 34/4420

Diaz, Jorge, and Uriz, Francisco.
    Mear contra el viento. In per. CDLA/CO, 21,
        julio/sept. 1974, p.8-50 (40/7258)

Díaz Vargas, Henry.
    Puño contra la roca, El. In per. UA/U, 51, 197,
        abril/junio 1976, p.109-115 (42/5958)

Diego, Celia de.
    Bajo el poncho azul (Buenos Aires : Casa Pardo, 1977;
        42/5959)

Discépolo, Armando.
    Amanda y Eduardo. In coll. 34/4011
    Babilonia. In coll. 34/4010
    Cremona. In coll. 34/4010
    Entre el hierro. In coll. 34/4011
    Fragua, La. In coll. 34/4011
    Giácomo. In coll. 34/4010
    Hombres de honor. In coll. 34/4011
    Levántate y anda. In coll. 34/4011
    Mateo-Stéfano (Buenos Aires : Editorial Kapelusz, 1976;
        40/7259)
    Movimiento continuo, El. In coll. 34/4011
    Muñeca. In coll. 34/4011
    Mustafá. In coll. 34/4011
    Organito, El. In coll. 34/4011
    Patria nueva. In coll. 34/4011
    Relojero. In coll. 34/4011
    Stéfano. In coll. 34/4011
    Vértigo, El. In coll. 34/4011

Domingos, Anselmo.
    Maria da fé. In per. RTB, num. 393, m/j '73 (40/7642)

Domingos, José and Serra, Silvano.
    Vida e obra de Manuá (Rio, 1971; 38/7536)

Domínguez, Franklin.
    Se busca un hombre honesto (Santo Domingo, 1965;
        30/3871a)

Dorr, Nicolás.
    Agitado pleito entre un autor y un ángel (La Habana :
        Instituto Cubano del Libro, 1973; 38/7167)
    Pericas, Las. In anthol. 30/3886

Dragún, Osvaldo.
    Amasijo, El see under new title Un maldito domingo
    Amoretta (Buenos Aires : Ediciones del Carro de Tespis,
        1965; 32/4422)
    Heroica de Buenos Aires (La Habana : Casa de las
        Americas, 1966; 30/3872; also Buenos Aires :
        Editorial Astral, 1967; 32/4423)
    Historia con cárcel. In anthol. 38/7159
    Historia del hombre que se cobirtió en perro. In
        anthol. 34/4047; in English as Man who turned into a
        dog in anthol. 00/4
    Historias para ser contadas. In anthol. 40/7314
    Los de la mesa diez. In anthol. 38/7171 and 40/7314
    Milagro en el mercado. In coll. 34/4012
    Un maldito domingo! (under title "El Amasijo", Buenos
        Aires : Calatayud Editor, 1968; 32/4421); also in
        coll. 34/4012; also in anthol. 42/5986
    Y nos dijeron que éramos inmortales. In coll. 34/4012;
        in English as And they told us we were immortal in
        anthol. 00/9

Dürst, Walter G.
Dez para as sete   (Rio : Editôra Letras e Artes, 1965;
        30/4204)
Rosa lúbrica   (Rio : Paz e terra, 1978; 42/6364)
Urna: cenas da vida subdesenvolvida, A   (São Paulo :
        Editôra Brasiliense, 1967; 36/7147)

Echevarría Loria, Arturo.
Espera, La.   In anthol. 32/4459

Eichelbaum, Samuel.
Guapo del 900, Un.   In anthol. 38/718
Pájaro de barro.   In coll. 30/3873
Vergüenza de querer.   In coll. 30/3873

Elizalde, Fernando de.
Sombrero de guindas   (Buenos Aires : Casa Impresora
        Francisco A. Colombo, 1977; 42/5960)

Emery, Milton de Moraes.
Começo é sempre fácil o difícil é depois   (Rio :
        Ministério da Educação e Cultura, Serviço
        Nacional de Teatro, 1968; 40/7618)

Endara, Ernesto.
Bandera, Una.   In per. LNB/L, 262, dic. 1977, p.111-122
        (42/5961)

Enríquez Gamón, Efraín.
Agonía del héroe, La   (Asunción : Editorial el
        Gráfico, 1977; 42/5962)

Escobar, Carlos Henrique de.
Caixa de cimento, A   (Rio : Civilização Brasileira,
        1978; 42/6365)
Engano, O.   In anthol. 42/6366

Espinosa Medrano, Juan de.
Hijo pródigo, El.   In anthol. 38/6449

Estevanell, Justo Esteban.
Impacto, El   (La Habana : Editorial Arte y Literatura,
        1976; 42/5963)

Esteve, Patricio.
Gran histeria nacional, La   (Buenos Aires : Editorial
        Talia, 91973; 38/7168)

Estorino, Abelardo.
Casa vieja, La.   In anthol. 32/4426
Peine y el espejo, El.   In anthol. 30/3886
Robo del cochino, El   (La Habana : Ediciones Revolución,
        1964; 30/3874)Fabian, Wanda.
Perda irreparável   (Rio : Editôra Letras e Artes, 1965;
        30/4205)

Farias Brasini, Mário.
    Quarta-feira, sem falta, lá em casa. In per. RTB, num.
        432, n/d '79 (40/7642)

Felipe, Carlos.
    Chino, El. In coll. 34/4013
    Compadres, Los. In coll. 34/4013
    Réquiem por Yarini (Miami, USA : Ediciones Calesa, 1978;
        42/5964). Also in coll. 34/4013
    Travieso Jimmy, El. In coll. 34/4013

Fernandes, Millôr.
    Bons temps, hein?! (Porto Alegre : L&PM Editores, 1979;
        42/6367)
    Flávia, cabeça, tronco e membros (Porto Alegre : L&PM
        Editores, 1977; 42/6368)
    Homem do princípio ao fim, O (Porto Alegre : L&PM
        Editores, 1978; 42/6369)
    Pigmaleoa (Rio, Ministério da Educação e Cultura,
        Serviço Nacional de Teatro, 1973; 38/7537)

Fernandes, Millôr, jt. auth. see under Rangel, Flávio.

Fernandez de Lizardi, José Joaquín.
    Dialogos del pensador, Los. In anthol. 32/4486

Fernández, Francisco F.
    Bautizo, El. In anthol. 40/7280
    Retórica y poética. In anthol. 40/7280

Fernández, Francisco F., jt. auth. see under Pequeño, P. N.

Fernández Vilaros, F.
    Negros catedráticos, Los. In anthol. 40/7280

Ferrari Amores, Alfonso.
    Arrimo de Puercoespines. In anthol. 34/4014
    Problema del oficial, El (Buenos Aires : Editorial Talia,
        1969; 34/4015)
    Toma de la bohardilla, La (Buenos Aires : Ediciones del
        Carro de Tespis, 1963; 34/4016)

Ferrari, Juan Carlos.
    Nata, La. In anthol. 34/4014

Ferreira, Helvécio.
    História do grito, A. In per. RTB, num. 389, s/o '72
        (40/7642)

Ferrer, Rolando.
    Próceres, Los. In anthol. 30/3886

Ferreti, Aurelio.
    Farsa sin público. In anthol. 34/4014

Figueiredo, Guilherme.
    Cara & coroa. In coll. 38/7539
    Deus dormiu lá em casa, Um (Rio : Ministério da
        Educação e Cultura, Serviço Nacional de Teatro,
        1973; 40/7619). Also in coll. 30/4206
    Fantasmas, Os. In coll. 30/4206
    Fim-de-semana. In coll. 38/7539
    Juízo final. In coll. 38/7539
    Maria da ponte (Rio : Ministério da Educação e
        Cultura, Serviço Nacional de Teatro, 1970; 38/7538)
    Meu Tio Alfredo. In coll. 38/7539

    Muito curiosa história da Virtuosa Matrona de Efeso, A.
        In coll. 30/4206
    Princípio de Arquimedes, O. In coll. 38/7539
    Rapôsa e as uvas, A. In coll. 30/4206
    Visita, Uma. In coll. 38/7539

Filippis, Jorge.
    Hijos de un drama, Los (Buenos Aires : Ediciones
        Kargieman, 1975; 40/7261)

Filloy, Juan.
    Tragedia del tiempo que transcurre y del dolor que no se
        aleja (Río Cuarto, Argentina : Talleres Gráficos
        Macció Hermanos, 1971; 36/6768)

Florit, Eugenio.
    Mujer sola, Una. In per. EX, 7:4, invierno 1973,
        p.73-179 (40/7262)

França Júnior, Joaquim José da.
    Caiu o ministério (Rio : Ministério da Educação e
        Cultura, Serviço Nacional de Teatro, 1972; 40/7620)

Francovich, Guillermo.
    Como los gansos [radio adaptation] In anthol.
        38/7291
    Puñal en la noche, Un. In anthol. 34/4046

Frank, Miguel.
    Hombre del siglo. In English as Man of the century in
        anthol. 00/3

Fuentes, Carlos.
    Todos los gatos son pardos (México : Siglo XXI
        Editores, 1970; 32/4427). Also in coll. 34/4017
    Tuerto es Rey, El. In coll. 34/4017Galich, Manuel.

Galich, Manuel.
    Miel amarga o al oso colmenero. In per. CDLA/CO, 24,
        abril/junio 1975 (40/7255)
    Mister John Ténor y yo. In per. CDLA/CO, abril/junio
        1976, p.27-111 (40/7263)
    Mugre, La. In coll. 42/5966

Galich, Manuel, cont'd.
Ortaet ed apor, o para leer al revés. In per. CDLA/CO,
26, enero/marzo 1976, p.77-93 (40/7264)
Papá natas. In coll. 42/5966
Pascual Abah. In coll. 42/5966; also in per. CDLA/CO,
3:6, enero/marzo 1968 (32/4428)
Pescado indigesto, El. In coll. 42/5966
Puedelotodo vencido o el gran Gukup-Cakish (La Habana :
Editorial Gente Nueva, 1978; 42/5965). Also in per.
CDLA/CO, 29, julio/sept. 1976 (40/7256)
Tren amarillo y otras obras, El. In coll. 42/5966
Ultimo cargo, El. In coll. 42/5966; also in per.
CDLA/CO, 20, abril/junio 1974, p.83-102 (40/7265)

Galindo, Alejandro.
Y la mujer hizo al hombre. In anthol. 40/7285

Gallegos, Daniel.
Colina, La (San José : Editorial Costa Rica, 1969;
32/4429). Also in anthol. 34/4046 and 40/7277
Profanos, Los. In per. RCR, 5:14, junio 1969 (32/4458)

Gambaro, Griselda.
Campo, El (Buenos Aires : Ediciones Insurrexit, 1967
(32/4430); in English as Camp in anthol. 00/8
Desatino, El (Buenos Aires : Centro de Experimentación
Audiovisual del Instituto Torcuato di Tella, 1965;
30/3875). Also in coll. 42/5967
Paredes, Las. In coll. 42/5967
Siameses, Los (Buenos Aires : Ediciones Insurrexit,
1967; 30/3876). Also in coll. 42/5967; also in
anthol. 42/5986
Sólo un aspecto. In per. UV/PH, 8, oct./dic. 1973,
p.52-72 (38/7169)

Gandara, Enrique.
Teatro de las tres carátulas, El (Buenos Aires :
Editorial Central, 1977; 42/5968)

Gangá, C.
Ajiaco; o, La Boda de Pancha Jutía y Canuto Raspadura,
Un. In anthol. 40/7280

Gann, Myra.
Amigos para siempre. In 38/7162

García Guerra, Iván.
Don Quijote de todo el mundo. In anthol. 34/4040 and
36/6795

García, Iván.
Fábula de los cinco caminantes. In anthol. 34/4047

García Guerra, Iván.
    Don Quijote de todo el mundo [radio adaptation]   In anthol.
        38/7291

García Jaime, Luis.
    Lágrimas y sonrisas.   In anthol. 38/7202

García Márquez, Gabriel.
    Tiempo de morir.   In per. INBA/CBA, 9, mayo/junio 1966
        (30/3877)

García Ponce, Juan.
    Doce y una, trece.   In anthol. 34/4023
    Feria distante, La.   In per. CV, 51/52, 1965, p.821-830
        and 52/53, 1966, p.846-845 (32/4431)
    Trazos.   In coll. 40/6604

García Ponce, Juan and Gurrola, Juan José.
    Tajimara.   In per. CV, 59/60, 1966/1967, p.1044-1052
        (32/4432)

García Saldaña, Parménides, jt. auth. see under Tovar, Juan.

García Velloso, Enrique.
    Mamá Culepina   (Buenos Aires : Libréria Huemul, 1974;
        38/7170)

Garibay, Ricardo.
    Crema chantilly.   In coll. 42/5969
    Gap.   In coll. 42/5969
    Guerra, La.   In coll. 42/5969
    Juegos de odio.   In coll. 42/5969
    Prisionera, La.   In coll. 42/5969

Garro, Elena.
    Arbol, El   (México, Rafael Peregrina Editor, 1967;
        30/3878)
    Felipe Angeles.   In per. CO, 8, otoño 1967, p.1-35
        (32/4432a)
    Perros, Los.   In anthol. 30/3857
    Señora en su balcón, La.   In anthol. 34/4023 and
        34/4047

Gaviria, José Enrique.
    Caminos en la niebla.   In coll. 42/5970
    Ejército de hormigas.   In coll. 42/5970
    Kaiyou.   In coll. 42/5970
    Llanto de los muertos, El.   In coll. 42/5970
    Sombra siguió adelante, La.   In coll. 42/5970

Gemba, Oraci.
    Como revisar um marido Oscar.   In anthol. 42/6381

Gentile, Guillermo.
    Hablemos a calzón quitado   (Ediciones Latinoamericanas,
        n.d.; 36/6769).   Also in anthol. 40/7314

Ghiano, Juan Carlos.
    Abanico de Venecia, El. In coll. 32/4434
    Antiyer. In coll. 32/4433 and 42/5971
    Corazón de tango. In coll. 32/4433 and 42/5971
    Desmemoriados, Los. In coll. 36/6770
    Devoradores, Los. In coll. 36/6770
    Duelo por su excelencia. In coll. 32/4434
    Extraviados, Los. In coll. 36/6770
    Narcisa Garay, mujer para llorar. In coll. 42/5971;
        also in anthol. 38/7171
    Nunca estaremos solas. In coll. 32/4434
    Pañuelo de llorar. In coll. 32/4434
    Protegidos, Los. In coll. 36/6770
    R.S.I.V.P. In coll. 32/4434
    Refugiados, Los. In coll. 36/6770
    Sirvientes, Los. In coll. 36/6770
    Testigos, Los. In coll. 36/6770
    Vestida de novia. In coll. 32/4434

Gil Gilbert, Enrique.
    Sangre, las velas y el asfalto, La. In anthol. 38/7202

Gill Camargo, Roberto.
    Última estación, A. In anthol. 42/6381

Glissant, Edouard.
    Monsieur Toussaint (Paris, Editions du Seuil, 1961;
        34/4299)

Góes, Yara Ferraz de.
    Estigma (Rio : Editora Fon Fon, 1973; 38/7540)

Goldenberg, Jorge.
    Relevo 1923 (La Habana : Casa de las Americas, 1975;
        40/7266)

Gomes Dias, Alfredo.
    Berço do herói, O (Rio : Editôra Civilação
        Brasileira, 1965; 30/4206a)
    Invasão, A. In coll. 38/7541
    Odorico, O Bem-Amado. In coll. 38/7541
    Pagador de promessas, O. In coll. 38/7541; in English
        as Payment as pledged in anthol. 00/9
    Primícias, As (Rio : Civilização Brasileira, 1978;
        42/6370)
    Santo Inquérito, O (Rio : Civilização Brasileira,
        1966; 32/4871). Also in coll. 38/7541
    Túnel, O. In coll. 38/7541; also in anthol. 42/6366
    Vamos soltar os demônios. In coll 38/7541

Gomes Dias, Alfredo and Gullar, Ferreira.
    Dr. Getúlio, sua vida e sua glória (Rio :
        Civilização Brasileira, 1968; 36/7148). Also in
        coll. 38/7541

Gomes, Roberto.
    Casa fechada, A (Rio : Ministério da Educação e
        Cultura, Serviço Nacional de Teatro, 1973; 40/7622)

Gómez de Avellaneda, Gertrudis.
    Baltasar. In anthol. 40/7268 and 40/7303
    Hija de las flores, La. In coll. 30/3879; also in
        anthol. 40/7303
    Millonario y la maleta, El. In coll. 30/3879
    Munio Alfonso. In coll. 30/3879; also in anthol.
        40/7268
    Saúl. In coll. 30/3879
    Tres amores. In anthol. 40/7268

Gómez Masía, Román, jt. auth. see under Monner Sans, José
    María.

Gondim Filho, Isaac.
    Grande estiagem, A (Rio : Ministério de Educação e
        Cultura, Serviço Nacional de Teatro, 1973; 38/7542)

González Bocanegra, Francisco.
    Vasco Núñez de Balboa. In anthol. 36/6779

González Caballero, Antonio.
    Medio pelo, El. In coll. 30/3880 and 36/6771; also in
        anthol. 30/3889a
    Señoritas a disgusto. In coll. 30/3880; also in
        anthol. 34/4023
    Una pura y dos con sal. In coll. 30/3880 and 36/6771

González Cajiao, Fernando.
    Huellas de un rebelde (Bogotá : Ediciones Tercer Mundo,
        1970; 34/4018)

Gonzalez Castillo, José, and Comorera, Juan.
    Puerto Madero. In anthol. 00/1

González Dávila, J.
    Gatos, Los. In anthol. 38/7161

González de Cascorro, Raúl.
    Hijo de Arturo Estévez, El (La Habana : Unión de
        Escritores y Artistas de Cuba, 1975; 40/7267)

González de Eslava, Fernán.
    Entremés del amorcado. In anthol. 38/7183
    Profeta Jonás, El. In anthol. 32/4486

González Delvalle, Alcibíades.
    Grito del Luisón, El (Asunción : Ediciones del Pueblo,
        1972; 36/6772)

González González, Sergio.
    Provisiones, Las (La Habana : Editorial Arte y
        Literatura, 1976; 42/5973)

González, Juan.
    Doce paredes negras (Río Piedras : Editorial Cultural,
        1978; 42/5972)

Gorostiza, Carlos.
    A qué jugamos? (Buenos Aires : Editorial Suamericana,
        1969; 32/4435)
    Color de nuestra piel, El. In anthol. 38/7183
    Juan y Pedro (Caracas : Monte Avila, 1976; 40/7270)
    Lugar, El (Buenos Aires : Editorial Sudamericana, 1972;
        36/6773)
    Mambrundia y Gasparindia. In coll. 40/7269
    Muerte de Platero, La. In coll. 40/7269
    Pan de la locura, El. In coll. 30/3881; also in
        anthol. 34/4046
    Platero y Titirilandia. In coll. 40/7269
    Prójimos, Los. In coll. 30/3881; in English as
        Prójimos in per. DRAMA, vol. 9, n. 2, Winter
        '70/'71
    Puente, El. In coll. 30/3881; also in anthol.
        38/7171 and 40/7271
    Quijotillo, El. In coll. 40/7269
    Vaquita triste, La. In coll. 40/7269

Gorostiza, Celestino.
    Color de nuestra piel, El. In English as Color of our
        skin in DRAMA, vol. 9, n. 3, Spring '71
    Malinche, La. In anthol. 34/4023

Gorostiza, Manuel Eduardo de.
    A ninguna de las tres. In anthol. 36/6779
    Contigo pan y cebolla. In anthol. 38/7183 and 40/7303

Granada, Nicolás.
    Al campo! In anthol. 34/4030 and 42/5953
    Atahualpa. In coll. 32/4436
    Bajo el parral. In coll. 32/4436
    Gaviota, La (Buenos Aires : Editorial Plus Ultra, 1973;
        38/7172)

Gregorio, Jesús.
    Canción para un día de julio. In per. CDLA/CO, 16,
        abril/junio 1973, p.41-75 (40/7272)

Grisolli, Paulo Afonso.
    Avatar. In coll. 40/7623; also in per. RTB, num. 408,
        n/d '75 (40/7642)
    Palatravi Malac Mic. In coll. 40/7623
    Temente Senhor Jó, O. In coll. 40/7623

Grupo Aleph.
    Erase una vez un rey. In per. CDLA/CO, 21, julio/sept.
        1974, p.68-83 (40/7273)

Grupo La Candelaria.
    Ciudad dorada, La. <u>In</u> per. CDLA/CO, 20, abril/junio
        1974 (40/7274)
    Guadalupe años sin cuenta (La Habana : Casa de las
        Americas, 1976; 40/7275)

Grupo Octubre.
    Toma, La. <u>In</u> per. CDLA/CO, 23, enero/marzo 1975,
        p.36-7<u>7</u> (40/7292)

Grupo Ollantay.
    S S 41. <u>in</u> per. CDLA/CO, 22, oct./dic. 1974, p.59-66
        (40/<u>7</u>260)

Guarnieri, Gianfrancesco.
    Botequim, ou céu sobra a chuva. <u>In</u> coll. 38/7544
    Castro Alves pede passagem (São Paulo : Palco &
        Platéia, 1971; 38/7543)
    Cimento, O. <u>In</u> coll. 42/6372
    Eles não usam black-tie (São Paulo : Editôra
        Brasiliense. 1966; 32/4872)
    Filho do Cão, O. <u>In</u> coll. 42/6372
    Gimba, presidente dos valentes (Rio : Ministério da
        Educação e Cultura, Serviço Nacional de Teatro,
        1973; 42/6371)
    Grito parado no ar, Um. <u>In</u> coll. 38/7544
    Janelas abertas. <u>In</u> anthol. 42/6366
    Ponto de partida (São Paulo : Editora Brasiliense,
        1976; 40/7624)
    Semente, A. <u>In</u> coll. 42/6372

Guérin, Mona.
    Oiseau de ces dames, L'. <u>In</u> coll. 36/7174
    Pension Vacher, La. <u>In</u> coll. 42/6541
    Pieuvre, La. <u>In</u> coll. 36/7174
    Sylvia. <u>In</u> coll. 42/6541

Guerra, Ruy, jt. auth. <u>see under</u> Hollanda, Chico Buarque de.

Guerrero, J. J.
    Guateque en la taberna un martes de carnaval, Un. <u>In</u>
        anthol. 40/7280

Gullar, Ferreira, jt. auth. <u>see under</u> Gomes, Alfredo Dias, and
    Vianna Filho, Oduvaldo.

Gullar, José Ribamar Ferreira.
    Rubi no umbigo, Um (Rio : Civilização Brasileira, 1978;
        42/6373)

Gunther, Luiz Eduardo, jt. auth. <u>see under</u> Coelho Júnior,
    Hélio Gomes.

Gurrola, Juan José, jt. auth. <u>see under</u> García Ponce, Juan.

Gutemberg, Luiz.
    Proceso Crispim, O. In per. RTB, num. 424, a '78
        (40/7642)

Gutiérrez, Eduardo.
    Juan Moreira (Buenos Aires : Ediciones Xanadú, 1973;
        38/7173). Also in anthol. 34/4030 and 38/7183

Gutiérrez, Ignacio.
    Mendigos, Los. In anthol. 30/3886

Guzmán Améstica, Juan.
    Wurlitzer, El. In per. EC/M, 19, invierno 1969,
        p.119-175 ($\overline{32}$/4437)

Halac, Ricardo.
    Estela de madrugada. In coll. 32/4438
    Fin de diciembre. In coll. 32/4438
    Segundo tiempo (Buenos Aires : Editorial Galerna, 1978;
        42/5974)

Heiremans, Luis Alberto.
    Abanderado, El. In anthol. 32/4424
    Año repetido, El. In per. EC/M, 3:1, 1965 (30/3882)
    Arpeggione. In per. EC/M, 3:1, 1965 (30/3882)
    Mar en la muralla, El. In per. EC/M, 3:1, 1965
        (30/3882)
    Palomar a oscuras, El. In per. UCH/A, 125:141/144,
        enero/dic. 1967, p.$\overline{148}$-183 (32/4439)
    Sigue la estrella. In anthol. 30/3931a
    Tony Chico, El. In per. EC/M, 16, otoño 1968,
        p.123-178 ($\overline{32}$/4440)

Helfgott, Sarina.
    Carta de Pierrot. In anthol. 38/7204
    Intermedio. In anthol. 38/7204
    Jaula, La. In coll. 32/4442
    Señorita Canario, La. In coll 32/4442

Henriquez, May.
    Sjon Pichiri (adapted from Molière). In per. AC, 5:4,
        1967 (30/3852)

Heredia, José María.
    Ultimos romanos, Los. In anthol. 42/6010

Herme, Juan Carlos, jt. auth. see under Pavlovsky, Eduardo.

Hernández, Luisa Josefina.
    Danza del urogallo múltiple. In anthol. 40/7285
    Huespedes reales, Los. In anthol. 34/4023
    Pavana de Aranzazú, La. In per. T, 1, oct./dic. 1975,
        p.13-37 (40/7276)
    Popol Vuh. In per. UV/PH, 10:40, 1966, p.699-734
        ($\overline{30/3883}$)

Hernández, Luisa Josefina, cont'd.
    Quetzalcóatl. In per. RBA, 20, marzo/abril 1968,
        p.38-58 (32/4443)

Herrera, Ernesto.
    Bella pinguito, La. In coll. 34/4019
    Caballo del comisario, El. In coll. 34/4019
    Estanque, El. In coll 34/4019
    León ciego, El. In coll. 34/4019
    Mala laya. In coll. 34/4019
    Moral de misia paca, La. In coll. 34/4019
    Pan nuestro, El. In coll. 34/4019

Herrera, Larry.
    Canario de la mala noche (Caracas : Editorial Ateneo de
        Caracas, 1979; 42/5975)

Hidalgo, Alberto.
    Volcándida (Buenos Aires : Editorial Kraft, 1967;
        30/3884)

Holanda, Nestor de.
    Bruxa, La (Rio : Irmãos Pongetti Editôres, 1962;
        30/4207)

Hollanda, Chico Buarque de and Guerra, Ruy.
    Calabar: o elogio da traição (Rio : Editora
        Civilização Brasileira, 1973; 38/7545)

Hollanda, Chico Buarque de and Pontes, Paulo.
    Gota d'água (Rio : Editora Civilização Brasileira,
        1975; 40/7626)

Ibargüengoitia, Jorge.
    Conspiración vendida, La. In per. INBA/CBA, 3,
        mayo/junio 1965, p.29-60 (30/3885)

Icaza, Alberto.
    Ancestral 66. In coll. 34/4058; also in anthol.
        34/4047
    Asesinato frustrado. In coll. 34/4058
    Escaleras para embrujar el tiempo. In coll. 34/4058

Imbert, Julio.
    Ángel en la mantequería, Un. In anthol. 34/4014
    Camila O'Gorman (Buenos Aires : Editorial Talía, 1968;
        32/4444)

Inclán, Federico S.
    Dos Juárez, Los. In anthol. 38/7175
    Frida Kahlo (México : Instituto Nacional de Bellas
        Artes, Depto. de Teatro, 1970; 38/7177)
    Última noche con Laura, La. In anthol. 34/4023

Jacintha, Maria.
   Convite à vida   (Rio : Editora Fon-Fon e Seleta, 1969;
      38/7546)
   Intermezzo da imortal esperança   (Rio : Ministério da
      Educação e Cultura, Serviço Nacional de Teatro,
      1973; 40/7627)
   Um não sei quê que nasce não sei onde   (Rio : Editôra
      Fon-Fon e Seleta, 1968; 32/4873)

Jesús Martínez, José de.
   Avaro y el mendigo, El.   In per. RCR, 5:14, junio 1969
      (32/4458)
   Enemigos.   In anthol. 36/6795

Jiménez Izquierdo, Joan.
   En busca de un hogar.   In anthol. 38/7162

Jockyman, Sérgio.
   "Lá".   In per. RTB, num. 381, m/j '71

Jodorowsky, Alexandro.
   Ensueño, El   (México : OPIC, 1967; 34/4020)
   Mole [excerpt of filmscript]   In per. T D R, vol. 14,
      n. 2, Winter '70
   Topo, El [filmscript]   (New York : Douglas Publ. Co.,
      1972)

Joffre, Sara.
   Obligación, Una.   In anthol. 38/7204

Jordão, Yolanda.
   Homens no palco   (Rio : Laudes, 1968; 36/7149)

Jorge, Miguel.
   Angélicos, Os.   In coll. 38/7547
   Visitante, O.   In coll. 38/7547

Júnior, França.
   Como se fazia um deputado.   In per RTB, num. 347, s/o
      '65

Kosta, Leonardo.
   Farsa del Aguijón, La.   In anthol. 38/7202

Kraly, Néstor.
   Balada maleva   (Buenos Aires : Talía, 1972; 40/7278)
   Ha muerto un payador   (Buenos Aires : Imprenta López,
      1968; 32/4446)
   No hay función.   In anthol. 30/3861

Laferrère, Gregorio de.
   Las de Barranco   (Buenos Aires : Editorial Plus Ultra,
      1966; 32/4447)

Lainez, Daniel.
    Timoteo se divierte. In coll. 42/5120aa

Lanz, Joaquín.
    Blue bird (adaptation). In anthol. 38/7203

Lanz, Joaquín, jt. auth. see under Ledesma, Oscar

Larreta, Antonio.
    Juan Palmieri (La Habana : Casa de las Americas, 1972;
        36/6774). Also in per. PRIA, 157, junio 1973,
        p.51-74 (38/7178)

Lasser, Alejandro.
    Catón y Pilato. In anthol. 34/4048

Laura, Ida.
    Senhora das Aguas e Senhor Dos Raios   (São Paulo, 1972;
        38/7548)

Lauten, Flora.
    Hermanos, Los. In per. CDLA/CO, 27, enero/marzo
        1976, p.19-38 (40/7279)

Ledesma, Oscar, and Lanz, Joaquín.
    Platero y yo [adaptation]. In anthol. 38/7187

Legido, Juan Carlos.
    Historia de Judíos   (Montevideo : Editorial Alfa,
        1969; 34/4021)

Leguizamón, Martiniano P.
    Calandria. In anthol. 34/4030

Lehmann, Marta.
    Evasión, La. In coll. 30/3887
    Fiesta, La. In coll. 30/3887
    Flagelados, Los. In coll. 30/3887
    Huida, La. In coll. 30/3887
    Lázaro, In coll. 30/3887
    Ofensiva, La. In coll. 30/3887
    Otra vez fedra. In coll. 30/3887
    Pfoximos, Los. In coll. 30/3887
    Secreto, El. In coll. 30/3887
    Su oportunidad. In coll. 30/3887
    Sumario, El. In coll. 30/3887
    Velo, El. In coll. 30/3887

Lemaitre, Eduardo.
    Ifigenia (Bogota : Instituto Colom,biano de Cultura,
        1973; 38/7180)

Leñero, Vicente.
    Albañiles, Los (México : Joaquín Mortiz Editor, 1970;
        34/4022) Also in anthol. 34/4023 and 36/6780

Leñero, Vicente, cont'd.
    Carpa, La. In anthol. 40/7285
    Compañeros. In anthol. 40/7284; also in per. D, vol.
        6, n. 2. m/a '70, p.14-27 (36/6776)
    Juicio, El. (México : Editorial Joaquín Mortiz, 1972;
        36/6777)
    Pueblo rechazado (México : Editorial; Joaquín
        Mortiz, 1969; 32/4448). Also in anthol. 40/7283

Lerner, Elisa.
    En el vasto silencio de Manhattan. In anthol.
        34/4048
    Envidia. In anthol. 42/6013
    Vida con mamá (Caracas : Monte Avila, 1976)

Levi, Clovis, and Pacheco, Tânia.
    Criminosa, greotesca, sofrida e sempre gloriosa
        caminhada de Alquí Cabá la Silva em busca de
        grande luz, A. In per. RTB, num. 398, m/a '74
        (40/7642)
    Se chavesse vocês estragavam todos (Europa Empresa
        Gráfica e Editora, 1977; 42/6374)

Libre Teatro Libre.
    Contratanto. In per. PRIA, 161, oct. 1973, p.51-61
        (38/7181)
    Fin del camino, El. In anthol. 42/6011; also excerpt
        in per. CU, 5, junio/julio 1975 (38/7182)
    Miguel. In per. CU, 5, junio/julio 1975 (38/7182)

Lima, Edy.
    Farsa da esposa perfeita, A (Porto Alegre : Editora
        Garatuja, 1976; 40/7628)

Lima, Stella Leonardos da Silva.
    Ifigênia de ouro. In coll. 36/7150 and 38/7549
    Jambinho do contra. In per. RTB, num. 381, m/j '71
    Maria do mar. In coll. 36/7150 and 38/7549

Lino Cayol, Roberto.
    Pompas de jabón; o el veraneo de Don Ponciano. In
        anthol. 42/5953

Lins, Osman.
    Auto do salão do automóvel. In coll. 40/7629
    Guerra do "Cansa-Cavalo" (Petrópolis : Editôra Vozes,
        1967; 30/4208)
    Lisbela e o prisionero (Rio : Editôra Letras e Artes,
        1964; 30/4209) Also in per. RTB, num. 334, j/a '63
    Mistério das figuras de barro. In coll. 40/7629
    Romance dos dois soldados de Herodes. In coll. 40/7629

Lizardi, Fernández de.
    Todos contra el payo. In anthol. 36/6779

Lizárraga, Andrés.
    Quiere Usted comprar un pueblo? In anthol. 32/4426
    Santa Juana de América (La Habana : Casa de las
        Américas, 1975; 40/7281)
    Torturador, El. In per. CDLA/CO, 15, enero/marzo 1973,
        p.95-121 (40/7282)

Llanos Aparicio, Luis.
    Leyenda de Supay Calle, La. In anthol. 42/5949

López Arellano, José.
    Estanque vacío, la palabra y el hombre, El. In per.
        NE, 3, julio/sept. 1972, p.61-71 (36/6778)
    Soplete, El. In anthol. 38/7161

López Pérez, Heriberto.
    Conversación en el parque. In coll. 42/5976
    Feliz entierro, canto de Juancito Verdades y la negra
        flora. In coll. 42/5976
    Leyenda de la calle de las mujeres, La. In coll.
        42/5976
    Última batalla de los vencidos en un día de terror y de
        miseria, La. In coll. 42/5976

López, Willebaldo.
    Arrieros con sus burros por la hermosa capital. In
        anthol. 38/7161
    Yo soy Juárez. In anthol. 38/7175 and 40/7286

Loredo, Rómulo.
    Guarandinga de Arroyo Blanco, La. In per. CDLA/CO, 24,
        abril/junio 1975 (40/7255)

Lourenço, Pasqual.
    Chuva de sorrisos, A. In per. RTB, num. 397, j/f 74
        (40/7642)
    Sorriso do Palhaço, O. In per. RTB, num. 388, j/a '72

Luaces, Joaquín Lorenzo.
    Aristodemo. In anthol. 42/6010
    Becerro de oro, El. In coll. 30/3888
    Mendigo rojo, El. In coll. 30/3888
    Zorra y Bulldog, A. In per. UCLV/I, 58, 1978, p.73-185
        (42/5977)

Luiz, Milton.
    Coelhinho Pitomba, O. In per. RTB, num. 378, n/d '70

Luna, J.
    Hacha, El. In anthol. 38/7161

Luna López, Estela.
    Eva no estuvo en el paraíso. In anthol. 38/7204

Luna, Nelson.
Gigante egoista, O. In per. RTB, num. 396, n/d '73
(40/7642)

Macaya Lahmann, Enrique.
Preludio a la noche. In anthol. 36/6790

Macêdo, Joaquim Manoel de.
Novo Otelo, O (Rio : Ministério da Educação e
Cultura, Serviço Nacional de Teatro, 1972; 40/7630)
Also in per RTB, num. 366, n/d '68
Pupila rica, Uma. In per RTB, num. 380, m/a '71

Machado de Assis, Joaquim Maria.
Quase ministro (Rio : Ministério da Educação e
Cultura, Serviço Nacional de Teatro, 1972; 40/7631)

Machado, María Clara.
Aprendiz de feiticeiro. In coll. 38/7550
Diamante do Grão-Mogol, O. In coll. 38/7550
Gata borralheira, A. In coll. 34/4252
Maria minhoca. In coll. 34/4252
Maroquinhas fru-fru. In coll. 34/4252
Menina e o vento, A. In coll. 34/4252
Pluft, o fantasminha. In anthol. 34/4040 and 36/6795;
in Spanish radio adaptation as Pluft el fantasmita
in anthol. 38/7291
Tribobó City. In coll. 38/7550

Macouba, Auguste.
Eia! Man-Maille la! (Paris : Pierre Jean Oswald, 1968;
34/4301)

Magalhães, Gonçalves de.
Poeta e a inquisição, O (Rio : Ministério da
Educação e Cultura, Serviço Nacional de Teatro,
1972; 40/7632)

Magalhães Júnior, Raymundo.
Canção dentro de pão. In per. RTB, num. 332, m/a
'63
Homem que fica, O. In per. RTB, num. 376, j/a '70
Imperador galante, O. In per. RTB, num. 388, j/a '72

Magalhães, Paulo de.
Coração não envelhece, O. In per. RTB, num. 333,
m/j '63

Magaña-Esquivel, Antonio.
Semilla del aire. In anthol. 34/4023

Magaña, Sergio.
Argonautas, Los (México : Instituto Nacional de Bellas
Artes, 1967; 32/4450)
Ensayando a Molière. In anthol. 30/3857 and 32/4486

Magaña, Sergio, cont'd.
    Moctezuma II. In per. INBA/CBA, 4:9, sept. 1963,
        p.69-108; 4:10, oct. 1963, p.73-112; 4:11, nov.
        1963, p.57-104 (30/3889)
    Pequeño caso de Jorge Lívido, El. In anthol. 34/4023

Maggi, Carlos.
    Apuntador, El. In anthol. 34/4047; also in per.
        PRIA, 96, marzo 1968, p.38-43 (36/6781)
    Biblioteca, La. In coll. 32/4452; in English as
        Library in anthol. 00/8
    Cuervo en la madrugada, Un. In per. CDLA/CO, 6:39,
        nov./dic. 1966, p.44-59 (30/3890)
    Esperando a Rodó. In coll. 32/4451
    Llamadas, Las. In coll. 32/4452
    Mascarada. In coll. 32/4451
    Motivo, Un. In per. N, 2:3/4, mayo 1964, p.67-80
        (36/6782)
    Noche de los ángeles inciertos. In coll. 32/4451
    Patio de la Torcaza, El. In coll. 32/4452; also in
        per. UV/PH, 45, enero/marzo 1968, p.147-196
        (36/6783)
    Trastienda, La. In coll 32/4452

Maia, Arthur.
    Dona Patinha vai ser Miss. In per. RTB, num. 355, j/f
        '67

Maia, Luiz, jt. auth. see under Almeida, Lyad de.

Maldonado Pérez, Guillermo.
    Por estos santos latifundios   (La Habana : Casa de las
        Américas, 1975; 40/7287)

Malfatti, Arnaldo.
    Tres berretines, Los   (Buenos Aires : Ediciones del Carro
        de Tespis, 1966; 30/3891)

Mancuso, Delmar.
    Negrinho do pastoreio: mito e ficção   (Porto Alegre :
        Editora Movimento, 1974; 38/7551)

Mantovani Abeche, Alfredo.
    Pesadelo. In anthol. 42/6381

Maranhão Filho, Luiz.
    Espanta gato: os da esquerda são devotos de Santo
        Antônio   (Rio : Ministério da Educação e
        Cultura, Serviço Nacional de Teatro; 40/7634)

Maranhão, José.
    Trigais de São Paulo, Os   (São Paulo : Empresa Gráfica
        da Revista dos Tribunais, 1972; 40/7633)

Marcos de Burros, Plínio.
    Barrela (São Paulo : Edições Simbolo, 1976; 40/7635)
    Dois perdidos numa noite suja (São Paulo : Global,
        1978; 42/6375)
    Homens de papel (São Paulo : Global, 1978; 42/6376)
    Navalha na carne. In coll. 42/6377
    Quando as máquinas param. In coll. 42/6377

Marechal, Leopoldo.
    Antígona veléz (Buenos Aires : Ediciones Citerea,
        1965; 30/3892)
    Batalla de José Luna, La (Santiago : Editorial
        Universitaria, 1970; 34/4024)

Marín, Gerard Paul.
    Retablo y guiñol de Juan Canelo. In anthol. 40/7312

Marín, Luis.
    Milagro del Señor de las Aguas, El. In anthol.
        38/7202

Marinuzzi, Raul.
    Hydromel dos avatares, O (Belo Horizonte : Informac
        Editora Gráfica, 1975; 40/7636)

Mármol, José.
    Cruzado, El. In anthol. 36/6764
    Poeta, El. In anthol. 36/6764

Marques Andrade, Euclides.
    Cão com gato. In per. RTB, num. 391, j/f '73
        (40/7642)

Marqués, René.
    Apartamiento, El. In coll. 36/6785; also in anthol.
        00/2
    Carnaval afuera, carnaval adentro (Rio Piedras :
        Editorial Antillana, 1971; 34/4025)
    Casa sin reloj, La. In coll. 38/6785
    David y Jonatán. In coll. 34/4026
    Hombre y sus sueños, El. In coll. 36/6785
    Mariana, o el alba. In anthol. 30/3933
    Muerte no entrará en palacio, La. In coll. 34/4027
        and 36/6785
    Niño azul para esa sombra, Un (Río Piedras : Editorial
        Cultural, 1972; 36/6784). Also in coll. 34/4027
        and 36/6785
    Sacrificio en el Monte Moriah (San Juan : Editorial
        Antillana, 1969; 32/4454)
    Sol y los Mac Donald, El. In coll. 36/6785
    Soles truncos, Los. In coll. 34/4027 and 36/6785;
        also in anthol. 32/4485 and 42/5986
    Tito y Berenice. In coll. 34/4026

Martí, José.
    Abdala. In anthol. 40/7268
    Amor con amor se paga. In anthol. 40/7268

Martínez Arango, Gilberto.
    Grito de los ahorcados, El. In anthol. 40/7238
    Proceso al Señor Gobernador. In per. CDLA/CO, 29,
        julio/sept. 1976 (40/7256)
    Zarpazo (Medellín : Univ. de Antioquia, 1973; 38/7184)

Martínez, José de Jesús.
    Caifás (Panamá : Ediciones Tareas, 1961; 30/3892a).
        Also in coll. 34/4029
    Caso Dios, El (Panamá : Ediciones Tareas, 1975; 40/7288
    Cero y van tres: tercer asalto (Panamá : Ministerio de
        Educación, Dirección de Cultura, 1970; 34/4028
    Enemigos (Panamá : Ediciones Tareas, 1962; 30/3892b).
        Also in anthol. 34/4040
    Guerra del banano, La (Panamá : Instituto Nacional de
        Cultura, 1976; 42/5978)
    Juicio final. In anthol. 00/7
    Retreta, La (Panamá : Ediciones de la Revista Tareas,
        1964; 30/3892c)
    Segundo asalto. In anthol. 34/4047

Martínez Payva, Claudio.
    Gaucho negro, El (Buenos Aires : Ediciones del Carro de
        Tespis, 1966; 30/3893)
    Lazo, El. In coll. 32/4455
    Ya tiene comisario el pueblo. In coll. 32/4455

Martínez Queirolo, José.
    Baratillo de la sinceridad, El. In coll. 38/7185
    Casa de modas, La. In anthol. 38/7202
    Casa del que dirán, La. In coll. 38/7185; also in
        anthol. 30/3932
    Cuestión de vida o muerte. In coll. 38/7185
    En alta mar. In coll. 38/7185
    Faltas justificadas, Las. In coll. 38/7185; also in
        anthol. 30/3932
    Goteras. In coll. 38/7185
    Habladores, Los. In coll. 38/7185
    Montesco y su señora. In coll. 38/7185
    QEPD. In coll. 38/7185; also in anthol. 38/7196;
        radio adaptation in anthol. 38/7291; in English as
        R. I. P. in anthol. 00/5
    Requiem por la lluvia. In coll. 38/7185
    Unos vrs. los otros, Los. In anthol. 34/4040

Mauricio, Julio.
    Depresión, La (Buenos Aires : Talía, 1970; 40/7289)
    Despido corriente, Un. In anthol. 36/6801
    Retratos, Los. In anthol. 38/7159

Medina, Roberto Nicolás.
     Cometa azul, La. In anthol. 30/3849
     Erase un viejo pirata (Buenos Aires : Editorial Plus
          Ultra, 1977; 42/5979)
     Larga espera, Una. In per. O, 1, julio 1968, p.25-35
          (34/4031)

Mejía, Medardo.
     Chapetones, Los. In anthol. 42/5120a

Mellado, M.
     Casa de Taita Andrés, La. In anthol. 40/7280

Mello, Zuleika.
     Profecia da cobra grande ou a trans-amazônica (Rio :
          Ministério da Educação e Cultura, Serviço
          Nacional de Teatro, 1972; 38/7552)

Melo, Fernando.
     Greta Garbo quem diria acabou no irajá. In per. RTB,
          400, j/a '74 (40/7642)

Mendes, Alejandro Samuel.
     En el valle de Oronqota (La Paz : Casa Municipal de la
          Cultura Franz Tamayo, 1978; 42/5980)

Méndez Ballester, Manuel.
     Arriba las mujeres. In anthol. 40/7313
     Bienvenido Don Goyito. In anthol. 30/3933 and 32/4485;
          radio adaptation in anthol. 38/7291
     Clamor de los surcos, El. In coll. 36/6786
     Hombre terrible del 87, El. In anthol. 40/7313
     Tiempo muerto. In coll. 36/6786

Méndez Quiñones.
     Jíbaros progresistas, Los. In anthol. 40/7303

Mendive, Rafael Maria de.
     Nube negra, La. In per. UCLV/I, 54. mayo/agosto 1976,
          p.157-180 (42/5981)

Menén Desleal, Alvaro.
     Circo y otras farsas, El. In anthol. 34/4047
     Dos ciegos en la muralla china. In per. A, 7,
          julio/agosto 1974, p.24-51 (38/7186)
     Luz negra. Inper. MN, 39/40, sept./oct. 1969, p.57-73
          (32/4456) and RCR, 5:14, junio 1969 (32/4458); in
          English as Black light in anthol. 00/5

Menéndez, Roberto Arturo.
     Ira del cordero, La. In anthol. 34/4040 and 36/6795;
          radio adaptation in anthol. 38/7291

Menezes, Constanza and Carreño, Virginia.
    Gobernador de la Roza   (San Juan : Editorial Sanjuanina,
        1966; 30/3894)

Menezes, Maria Wanderley.
    Amor na terra do cangaço, O.   In per RTB, num. 330,
        n/d '62
    Caminhos verdes do mar   (Rio : Serviço Nacional de
        Teatro, 1972)
    Madalena e Salomé   (Rio : Serviço Nacional de Teatro,
        19?)

Mertens, Federico.
    Carabina de Ambrosio, La.   In anthol. 42/5953

Milanés, José Jacinto.
    Conde Alarcos, El.   In anthol. 42/6010

Mohana, João.
    Por causa de Inês   (Rio : Livraria Agir Editora, 1971;
        38/7553)

Molleto, Enrique.
    Confesión, La.   In per. EC/M, 5:1, 1966, p.102-105
        (30/3895)
    Sótano, El.   In anthol.. 30/3931a

Mombrú, Maria.
    Mataron a un taxista   (Buenos Aires : Editorial Talía,
        1970; 34/4032)

Monasterios, Rubén.
    Lujuria.   In anthol. 42/6013

Monner Sans, José María and Gómez Masía, Román.
    Islas orcadas   (Buenos Aires : Ediciones del Carro de
        Tespis, 1968; 30/3895a)

Montaine, Eliseo, jt. auth. see under Tálice, Roberto A.

Montalvo, Juan.
    Descomulgado, El.   In coll. 42/5982
    Dictador, El.   In coll. 42/5982
    Granja.   In coll. 42/5982
    Jara.   In coll. 42/5982
    Leprosa, La.   In coll. 42/5982

Montaña, Antonio.
    Diálogo de truhanes, bribones y prudentes o la noche del
        día de San Francisco.   In per. RBA, 26,
        marzo/abril 1969, p.15-25 (36/6787)
    Tiempo de la trompeta.   In coll. 32/4457
    Tobías y el ángel.   In coll. 32/4457

Monteagudo, Bernardo.
    Diálogo entre Atawallpa y Fernando VII en los Campos
        Elíseos   (La Paz, 1973; 38/7188)

Monteiro, José Maria.
    Contraponto. In coll. 38/7554
    Girafinha das Arábias, Uma. In per. RTB, num. 393,
        m/j '73 (40/7642)
    Medalhas, As. In coll. 38/7554

Monteiro, Marília Gama.
    Era uma de verdade tiradentes   (Rio : Ministério da
        Educação e Cultura, Serviço Nacional de Teatro,
        1969; 38/7555)
    Ovo de Colombo, O (Rio : Ministério da Educação e
        Cultura, Serviço Nacional de Teatro, 1969; 38/7556)

Montes Huidobro, Matías.
    Gas en los poros. In anthol. 30/3886
    Sal de los muertos. La. In anthol. 34/4040 and 36/6795

Monti, Ricardo.
    Historia tendenciosa de la clase media argentina, de los
        extraños sucesos en que se vieron envueltos algunos
        hombres públicos, su completa dilucidación y otras
        escandalosas revelaciones. (Buenos Aires : Talía,
        1972; 40/7290)
    Noche con el Sr. Magnus e Hijos, Una (Buenos Aires :
        Talía, 1971; 34/4033)

Moock, A.
    Serpiente, La. In anthol. 38/7183

Mora, Juan Miguel de.
    Plaza de las tres culturas (México : Editores Asociados
        Mexicanos, 1978; 42/5983)

Moraes, Antônio Santos.
    Rei Zumbi. In coll. 32/4875
    Terra Sangra, A. In coll. 32/4875

Morales Alvarez, R.
    Proceso del oso, El. In anthol. 40/7280

Morales, Jacobo.
    Cinco sueños en blanco y negro (Río Piedras :
        Editorial Antillana, 1977; 42/5984)

Morales, José Ricardo.
    Hay una nube en su futuro. In anthol. 30/3931a

Moreira, Fernando.
    Reunião em família (São Luiz : Depto. de Cultura do
        Estado, 1969; 38/7557)

Morete, María Luisa.
En el vientre. In coll. 30/3896
Viaje al este. In coll. 30/3896
Vuelo en el crepúsculo, El. In coll. 30/3896

Moreyra, Alvaro.
Adão, Eva e outros membros da família (Rio :
Ministério da Educação e Cultura, Serviço
Nacional de Teatro, 1973; 38/7558)

Morris, Andrés.
Guarizama, El (Tegucigalpa : López y Cía, 1966;
30/3897). Also in coll. 34/4034
Miel del abejorro, La. In coll. 34/4034; also in
per. RCR, 5:14, junio 1969 (32/4458)
Oficio de hombres. In coll. 34/4034; also in anthol.
34/4040; radio adaptation in anthol. 38.7291

Mossi, Miguel Angel.
Ollantay. In anthol. 38/7183; also in per. FIRST, vol.
6, n. 1, Spring '67
Muello, Juan Carlos.
Guerra a las polleras. In coll. 42/5985
Que lindo es estar casado...y tener la suegra al lado.
In coll. 42/5985

Muniz, Lauro César.
Comédia atômica, A. In per. RTB, num. 379, j/f '71
Este ôvo é um galo. In per. RTB, num. 363, m/j
'68
Infidelidade ao alcance de todos, A. In per. RTB,
num. 371, s/o '69
Mito, O. In anthol. 42/6366
Morte do Imortal, A. In per. RTB, num. 391, j/f '73
Santo milagroso, O. In per. RTB, num. 356, m/a '67

Nalé Roxlo, C.
Pacto de Cristina. In anthol. 38/7183

Naranjo, Carmen.
Voz, La. In anthol. 36/6790

Nari, Fortunato E.
Habitante, El (Santa Fe : Librería y Editorial
Colmegna, 1973; 38/7189)

Navajas Cortés, Esteban.
Agonía del difunto, La (La Habana : Casa de las
Américas, 1976; 40/7291). Also in per. CDLA/CO,
29, julio/sept. 1976 (40/7256)

Navarro Carranza, Francisco.
Muerte en el bosque (México : Librería Porrúa, 1967;
30/3898)

Negri, Nilton.
    Bruxinha Dorotéia, A.   In per. RTB, num. 427, j/f '79
        (40/7642)

Neruda, Pablo.
    Fulgor y muerte de Joaquín Murieta, bandido chileno
        injusticiado en California el 23 de julio de 1853
        (Santiago : Empresa Editora Zig-Zag, 1966; 30/3898a;
        and Buenos Aires : Editorial Losada, 1974; 38/7190);
        in German as Glanz und Tod des Joaquin Murieta.
        In THEATER, n. 4, Apr. '71

Neto, Coelho.
    Patinho Torto, O.   In per. RTB, num. 341, s/o '64

Neves, João das.
    Leiteiro e a menina noite, O (Rio : Ministério da
        Educação e Cultura, Serviço Nacional de Teatro,
        1970; 38/7559)
    Quintal, O.   In anthol. 42/6366

Novión, Alberto.
    Primeros fríos, Los.   In anthol. 00/1
    Rincón de los caranchos, El.   In anthol. 00/1

Novo, Salvador.
    Coronel Astucia, El (adaptation).   In anthol. 38/7203
    Cuauhtémoc.   In anthol. 34/4023
    Ha vuelto Ulises.   In anthol. 30/3857
    In Ticitezcatl o el espejo encantado.   In anthol.
        40/7286

Novoa, Mario.
    Sistema, El.   In per. EX, 6:2, verano 1972, p.121-129
        (36/6788)

Nunes, Carlos Alberto.
    Estácio (São Paulo, Edições Melhoramentos, 1971;
        40/7637)

Nunes, Cassiano.
    Luvas de Ema, As (Rio : Livraria São José, 1973;
        40/7638)

Núñez, José Gabriel.
    Largo camino del Edén, El.   In per. VME/R, 32:199,
        agosto 1971, p.109-117 (36/6789)
    Peces del acuario, Los.   In anthol. 34/4048

Nuñez, Nicolás.
    Comedy of errors.   In anthol. 38/7187

Oliva, Felipe.
    Pelo en plena juventud, Un.   In anthol. 42/5987

Oliveira, Domingos de.
    História de muitos amôres, A. In coll. 34/4253
    Somos todos do jardim infância. In coll. 34/4253

Oliveira, Pernambuco de.
    Amanhã eu vou (Rio : Ministério da Educação e
        cultura, Serviço Nacional de Teatro, 1972; 38/7560)

Oliveira, Valdemar de.
    Terra adorada. In per. RTB, num. 416, m/a '77
        (40/7642)

Olmos, Carlos.
    Juegos fatuos. In anthol. 40/7286

Oporto, Walter.
    Ceremonia al pie del obelisco. In anthol. 40/7314

Orihuela, Roberto.
    Ramona. In anthol. 42/5987

Orozco Castro, Jorge.
    Germinal. In anthol. 32/4459

Ortega, Julio.
    Campana, La. In coll. 30/3899 and 42/5988; also in
        anthol. 34/4047
    Ceremonia. In coll. 42/5988
    Como cruzar una calle. In coll. 30/3899
    Intruso, El. In coll. 30/3899 and 42/5988
    Invasión de una calle. In coll. 42/5988
    Lazaro. In coll. 30/3899
    Ley, La. In coll. 30/3899 and 42/5988
    Mesa pelada. In coll. 42/5988
    Moros en la costa. In coll. 30/3899
    Mosto de los lagares, El. In coll. 30/3899
    Paraíso de los suicidas, El. In coll. 42/5988
    Pedir la palabra. In coll. 42/5988
    Perfecta soledad. In coll. 30/3899 and 42/5988
    Retorno, El. In coll. 42/5988
    Se vende cualquier cosa. In coll. 30/3899
    Sociedad anonima. In coll. 30/3899
    Varios rostros del verano. In coll. 42/5988; also in
        anthol. 30/3907

Orthof, Sylvia.
    Eu chovo, tu choves, ele chove. In per. RTB, num. 431,
        s/o '79 (40/7642)

Osorio, Luis Enrique.
    Amor de los escombros, El. In coll. 30/3900
    Creadores, Los. In coll. 30/3900
    Iluminado, El. In coll. 30/3900
    Ruta inmortal, La. In coll. 30/3900
    Tragedia íntima. In coll. 30/3900

Ospina, Sebastián.
     Huelga, La. In anthol. 40/7238

Pacheco, Carlos Mauricio.
     Diablo en el conventillo, El (Buenos Aires : Ediciones
          del Carro de Tespis, 1966; 30/3901); also in
          anthol. 00/1
     Tristes o gente oscura, Los. In anthol. 00/1

Pacheco, Tânia, jt. auth. see under Levi, Clóvis.

Pagano, José León.
     Astros, Los (Buenos Aires : Ediciones del Carro de
          Tespis, 1965; 30/3902)

Palant, Jorge.
     Griselda en la cuerda. In coll. 40/7293
     Vine a verte, Papá. In coll. 40/7293
     Visitas, Las. In coll. 40/7293

Palant, Pablo.
     Esta mujer mía (Buenos Aires : Ediciones del Carro de
          Tespis, 1966; 30/3903)
     María de los dos. In coll. 32/4460
     Piano y otros juegos, El. In coll. 32/4460

Pallottini, Renata.
     Crime da cabra, O. In per. RTB, num. 394, j/a '73
          (40/7642)
     Escorpião de Numância, O (São Paulo : Conselho
          Estadual de Cultura, Comissão Estadual de Teatro;
          38/7561)
     História do juiz, A. In per. RTB, num.407, s/o '75
          (40/7642)

Palomares, Francisco.
     Imagen de Juárez. In anthol. 38/7175

Paola Levín, Jorge di.
     Hernán (La Plata : Ediciones del Cuadrante, 1963)

Paoli, Carlos de.
     Chicos de Pérez, Los. In anthol. 00/1

Pardo y Aliaga, Felipe.
     Frutos de la educación. In coll. 34/4035
     Huérfana en chorrillos, Una. In coll. 34/4035

Parra, Nicanor.
     Todas las colorinas tienen pecas, o solo para mayores de
          cien años. In per. REAC, 2, 1972, p.80-108
          (36/6792)

Parrado, Gloria.
     Día en la agencia, Un. In coll. 32/4461

Parrado, Gloria, cont'd.
    Espera, La. In coll. 32/4461
    Juicio de Aníbal. In coll. 32/4461

Pasos, J. and Coronel Urtecho, José
    Chinfonía burguesa. In anthol. 40/7315

Pavlovsky, Eduardo A.
    Acto rápido, Un. In coll. 30/3905
    Alguien. In coll. 30/3905
    Espera trágica, La. In coll. 30/3905
    Mueca, La. (Buenos Aires : Talía, 1971; 40/7294).
        Also in coll 34/4051
    Robot, El. In coll. 30/3905
    Señor Galíndez, El. In per. PRIA, 179/181, verano
        1975, p.65-73 (40/7295)
    Somos. In coll. 30/3905
    Telarañas (Buenos Aires : Ediciones Búsqueda, 1976;
        40/7296)

Pavlovsky, Eduardo A. and Herme, Juan Carlos.
    Ultimo match (Buenos Aires : Talía, 1970; 40/7297)

Payró, Roberto Jorge.
    Mientraiga. In anthol. 42/5953

Paz, Octavio.
    Hija de Rappaccini, La. In anthol. 34/4023

Pedroso, Bráulio.
    Deus nos acuda, O. In coll. 40/7640
    Encontro no bar. In coll. 40/7640
    Fardão, O (Rio : Editôra Saga, 1967; 32/4876). Also
        in coll. 40/7640
    Fula do Bucalão, A. In coll. 40/7640
    Hienas, As. In coll. 40/7640
    Negócio, O. In coll. 40/7640
    Vida escrachada de Joana Martini e Baby Stompanato, O.
        In coll. 40/7640

Pelayo, Félix M.
    Fuego en las breñas (Buenos Aires : Ediciones del Carro
        de Tespis, 1965; 30/3906)

Peña, Edilio.
    Círculo, El. In coll. 40/7298
    Resistencia: o un extraño sueño sobre la tortura de
        Pablo Rojas. In coll. 40/7298

Peón y Contreras, José.
    Cabeza de uconor, La. In coll. 38/7192
    Gil González de Avila. In coll. 38/7192
    Hija del rey, La. In coll. 38/7192
    Por el joyel del sombrero. In coll. 38/7192

Pequeño, P. N. and Fernández, Francisco F.
    Negro Cheche; o, veinte años despues, El. In anthol.
        40/7280

Peregrina Corona, S.
    Desempleo, El. In anthol. 34/3996
    Volver a decir el mar. In anthol. 38/7161

Pérez-Carmona, Juan.
    Piedra libre. In anthol. 34/4040 and 36/6795
    Revolución de las macetas, La (Buenos Aires : Editorial
        Talía, 1966; 32/4462) Radio adaptation in
        anthol. 38/7291

Pérez Luna, Edgardo.
    Orfeo en las tinieblas. In anthol. 30/3907

Pérez Pardella, Agustín.
    Savonarola. In coll. 30/3908
    Strip-Tease: no matarás. In coll. 30/3908
    Víspera del alma, La. In coll. 30/3908

Pérez Rey, Lupe.
    Astucia femenina. In anthol. 32/4459

Petit de Murat, Ulises and Demichelli, Tulio.
    Espejo para la santa (Buenos Aires : Ediciones del Carro
        de Tespis, 1970; 34/4036)

Petraglia, Cláudio, jt. auth. see under Silveira, Miroel

Pfuhl, Oscar von.
    Arvore que andava, A. In coll. 34/4254
    Beterrabas do Sr. Duque, As. In coll. 34/4254
    Bomba do Chico Simão, A. In coll. 34/4254
    Elefantinho incomoda muita gente, Um. In coll. 34/4254
    Lôbo na cartola, Um. In 34/4254
    Romão e Julinha. In per. RTB, num. 382, j/a '71

Philoctête, René.
    Monsieur de Vastey (Port-au-Prince : Les Editions
        Fardin, 1975; 40/7781)

Pimentel, Altimar de Alencar.
    Auto de cobiça, O. In per. RTB, num. 370, j/a '70
    Construção, A (Rio : Ministério da Educação e
        Cultura, Serviço Nacional de Teatro, 1969;
        38/7562); also in per. RTB, num. 373, j/f '70
    Última lingada, A. In per. RTB, num. 415, jan. 77
        (40/7642)

Pineda, José.
    Marginados, Los (Santiago : Sociedad de Escritores de
        Chile, 1967; 30/3909)

Piñera, Virgilo.
     Dos viejos pánicos   (La Habana : Casa de las Américas,
          1968; 30/3909a)
     Estudio en blanco y negro. In anthol. 34/4047
     Falsa alarma. In anthol. 30/3886; radio adaptation
          in anthol. 38/7291

Pinheiro, Jair.
     Gato Playboy, O. In per. RTB, num. 377, s/o '70

Pinto, Gilberto.
     Fantasmas de Tulemón, Los   (Caracas : Monte Avila
          Editores, 1975; 38/7193)
     Hombre de la rata, El. In anthol. 34/4048

Pires, Meira.
     João Farrapo. In per. RTB, num. 342, n/d '64

Plá, Josefina.
     Fiesta en el río   (Asunción : Editorial Siglo XXI,
          1977; 42/5989)
     Historia de un número. In anthol. 34/4040 and
          34/4047; radio adaptation in anthol. 38/7291

Ponferranda, Juan Oscar.
     Carnaval del diablo, El. In coll. 34/4037
     Gran nido verde, Un. In coll. 34/4037
     Pastores, Los. In coll. 34/4037
     Trigo es de Dios, El   (Buenos Aires : Ediciones del Carro
          de Tespis, 1967; 32/4464)

Pongetti, Henrique.
     Amanhã se não chover. In per. RTB, num. 336, n/d '63
     Zefa entre os homens. In per. RTB, num. 331, j/f '63

Pontes, Paulo.
     Doutor Fausto da Silva. In per. RTB, num. 405, m/j '75
          (40/7642)

Pontes, Paulo, jt. auth. see under Hollanda, Chico Buarque de.

Porfírio, Pedro.
     Belo Burguês, O (Rio : Europa, 1978; 42/6378)

Porto, Oswaldo de.
     Rômulo e o maribondo (Rio : Princeps Gráfica e
          Editôra, 1968; 34/4255)

Portocarrero, Elena.
     Corcova, La. In coll. 32/4465
     Hoy no, mañana tampoco. In coll. 32/4465

Prata, Mário.
     Cordão umbilical, O. In per. RTB, num. 390, n/d '72
          (40/7642)

Qorpo Santo, José Joaquim de Campos Leão.
    Assovio, Um. In coll. 34/4256
    Certa entidade em busca de outra. In coll. 34/4256
    Credor da fazenda nacional, Um. In coll. 34/4256
    Hoje sou um; e amanhã outro. In coll. 34/4256
    Lanterna de fogo. In coll. 34/4256
    Mateus e Mateusa. In coll. 34/4256
    Parto, Um. In coll. 34/4256
    Relações naturais, As   (Rio : Ministério da Educação
        e Cultura, Serviço Nacional de Teatro, 1972;
        38/7564). Also in coll. 34/4256

Queiroz, Rachel de.
    Beata Maria de Egito, A.   (Rio : Ministério da
        Educação e Cultura, Serviço Nacional de Teatro,
        1973; 40/7641)

Queiroz Telles, Carlos.
    Bolsinha magica de Marly Emboaba, A.   In per. RTB, num.
        430, j/a '79 (40/7642)
    Frei Caneca.   In per. RTB, num. 396, n/d '73 (40/7642)
    Muro de arrimo.   In per. RTB, num. 412, j/a '76
        (40/7642)

Quintana, J. M. de.
    Trichina, La.   In anthol. 40/7280

Quintero, Héctor.
    Contigo pan y cebolla   (La Habana : Ediciones
        Revolución, 1965; 32/4466)

Quintero, Lucía.
    1x1=1, pero 1+1=2. In anthol. 34/4048

Rabinovich, José.
    Con pecado concebida   (Buenos Aires : Ediciones del Carro
        de Tespis, 1975; 42/5991)

Radde, Ronald.
    Apaga a luz e faz de conta que estamos bebados.   In
        per. RTB, num. 397, j/f '74 (40/7642)
    B...em cadeira de rodas.   In per. RTB, num. 427, j/f
        '79 (40/7642)
    Transe.   In per. RTB, num. 389, s/o '72 (40/7642)

Ramírez Farías, Carlos.
    Palito y Godsuno   (Caracas : Ediciones MAPA, 1976;
        40/7299)

Ramírez Heredia, Rafael.
    Dentro de estos ocho muros.   In anthol. 42/5990

Ramos, J. A.
    Tembladera.   In anthol. 38/7183

Rangel, Flávio and Fernandez, Millôr.
    Liberdade, liberdade (Rio : Editôra Civilização
        Brasileira, 1965; 30/4210)

Razo, Mario del, adapter see under Cuéllar, José Tomás de.

Rebolledo, Efrén.
    Aguila que cae, El. In coll. 30/3909b

Rechani Agrait, Luis.
    Cómo se llama esta flor? In anthol. 30/3933
    Mi señoría (Barcelona : Ediciones Rumbos, 1968;
        32/4467). Also in anthol. 32/4485
    Todos los ruiseñores cantan (Barcelona : Ediciones
        Rumbos, 1966; 32/4468)

Reguera Saumell, Manuel.
    General Antonio estuvo aqui, El. In anthol. 30/3886
    Recuerdos de tulipa (La Habana : Ediciones Revolución,
        1965; 30/3910)

Rengifo, César.
    Buenaventura Chatarra. In coll. 30/3911
    Esquina del Miedo, La. In anthol. 34/4048
    Estrellas sobre el crepúscolo. In coll. 30/3911
    Fiesta de los moribundos, La. In coll. 34/4038
    Hombres de los cantos amargos, Los. In coll. 34/4038
        and 42/6009
    Lo que dejó la tempestad. In coll. 42/6009
    Manuelote [radio adaptation] In anthol. 38/7291
    María Rosario Nava (Mérida : Univ. de los Andes,
        Ediciones del Rectorado, 1964; 32/4469)
    Medalla para las conejitas, Una. In per. E, 1, p.43-53
        (32/4470) and CDLA/CO, 22, oct./dic. 1974 (40/7300)
    Raudal de los muertos cansados, El. In coll. 42/6009
    Sonata del alba, La. In per. CDLA/CO, 22, oct./dic.
        1974 (40/7300)
    Tal Ezequiel Zamora, Un. In coll. 42/6009
    Torres y el viento, Las. In coll. 42/6009; also in
        anthol. 34/4040 and 36/6795
    Vendaval amarillo, El. In coll. 30/3911 and 42/6009

Requena, María Asunción.
    Ayayema. In anthol. 32/4424

Retes, Ignacio.
    Hombres de cielo, Los: crónica dramática sobre
        Bartolomé de las Casas (México : Instituto
        Tecnológico y de Estudios Superiores de Monterrey,
        1966; 30/3912)
    Viento sur. In anthol. 38/7206

Reuben, William.
    Teófilo Amadeo: una biografía. In anthol. 40/7277

Revueltas, José.
   Cuadrante de la Soledad, El   (México : Editorial Novaro,
      1971; 36/6793)

Rey, Marcos.
   Parceiros, Os.   In per. RTB, num. 423, m/j '78
      (40/7642)
   Próxima vítima, A.   In per. RTB, num. 358, j/a '67

Reyes, Carlos José.
   Fiesta de los muñecos, La.   In per. CDLA/CO, num. 24,
      abril/junio 1975 (40/7255)
   Metamorfosis.   In anthol. 34/4040
   Viejos baúles empolvados que nuestros padres nos
      prohibieron abrir, Los   (Bogotá : Ministerio da
      Educación Nacional, Instituto Colombiano de Cultura,
      1973; 38/7194)

Reyes de la Maza, Luis.
   Déjame salir.   In per. UV/PH, 12, oct./dic. 1974
      (38/7195)

Reyes García, Ismael.
   Ella o yo!   In coll. 42/5993
   Tramoyistas, Los.   In coll 42/5993

Reyes Ortiz, Félix.
   Lanzas, Las.   In coll. 42/5994
   Plan de una representación.   In coll. 42/5994

Reyes Palacios, F.
   Colmillos de la ballena, Los.   In anthol. 38/7161

Rial, José Antonio.
   Muerte de García Lorca, La   (Caracas : Monte Avila,
      1976; 40/7310)

Ribeyro, Julio Ramón.
   Caracoles, Los.   In coll. 40/7302
   Confusión en la prefectura.   In coll. 40/7302
   Fin de semana.   In coll. 40/7302
   Santiago, el pajarero.   In coll. 40/7302
   Sótano, El.   In coll. 40/7302
   Ultimo cliente, El.   In coll. 40/7302
   Uso de la palabra, El.   In coll. 40/7302

Rio, João do.
   Bela Madame Vargas, A   (Rio : Ministério da Educação
      e Cultura, Serviço Nacional de Teatro, 1973;
      40/7643)

Rio, Marcela del.
   Pulpo, El.   In anthol. 40/7284

Rivarola Matto, José María.
    Fin de Chipí González. In English as Fate of Chipí
        González _in_ anthol. 00/3

Rivas, Ana.
    30 dineros   (Buenos Aires : Ediciones Dintel, 1972;
        42/5995)

Rivera Saavedra, Juan.
    Humanoides, Los. _In_ anthol. 34/4023

Robles, J. Humberto.
    Desarraigados, Los. _In_ anthol. 34/4023

Rocha, Aurimar.
    Genro que era nora, O. _In_ per. RTB, num. 429, m/j '79
        (40/7642)
    Jojo de verdade, O. _In_ per. RTB, num. 409, j/f '76
        (40/7642)

Rocha Filho, Ruben.
    Diário de um louco   (Rio : Editôra Fon-Fon e Seleta,
        1968; 34/4257)

Rocha Miranda, Edgar da.
    Estranho, O. _In_ per. RTB, num. 402, n/d '74 (40/7642)

Rodrigues, Elza Corrêa.
    Estória da Rosa Princípe, A. _In_ per. RTB, num. 387,
        m/j '72

Rodrigues, José Maria.
    Volta do prometido, A. _In_ per. RTB, num.422, m/a '78
        (40/7642)

Rodrigues, Nelson.
    7 Gatinhos, Os. _In_ coll. 32/4877
    Album de família. _In_ coll. 32/4877
    Anjo negro. _In_ coll. 32/4877
    Beijo no asfalto, O. _In_ coll. 32/4877
    Bôca de ouro. _In_ coll. 32/4877
    Bonitinha mas ordinário (São Paulo : Editora
        Brasiliense, 1965; 38/7566). _Also in_ coll.
        32/4877
    Dorotéia. _In_ coll. 32/4877
    Falecida, A. _In_ coll. 32/4877; _also in_ per. RTB,
        num. 337, j/f '64
    Mulher sem pecado, A. _In_ coll. 32/4877
    Perdoa-me por me traíres. _In_ coll. 32/4877
    Senhora dos afogados. _In_ coll. 32/4877
    Tôda nudez será castigada (Rio : Distribuidora Record;
        38/7567). _Also in_ coll. 32/4877
    Valsa No. 6. _In_ coll. 32/4877

Rodrigues, Nelson, cont'd.
    Vestido de noiva   (Rio : Ministério da Educação e
        Cultura, Serviço Nacional de Teatro, 1973;
        38/7568). Also in coll. 32/4877
    Viúva, porém honesta. In coll. 32/4877

Rodríguez, Azucena, adapter see under Cuéllar, José Tomás
    de.

Rodríguez Castelo, Hernán.
    Casandra, el payaso y el vagabundo. In anthol. 38/7196

Rodríguez Galván, Ignacio.
    Muñoz, visitador de México. In coll. 36/6794; also
        in anthol. 36/6779 and 40/7303
    Privado del virrey, El. In coll. 36/6794

Rodríguez, Jorge Mario.
    Derrumbe, El. In coll. 42/5996
    Otros, Los. In coll. 42/5996

Rodríguez Muñoz, Alberto.
    Biógrafo (Buenos Aires : Ediciones del Carro de Tespis,
        1971; 34/4039)
    Melenita de oro. In coll. 30/3913
    Tango del Angel, El. In coll. 30/3913
    Tangos de Orfeo, Los. In coll. 30/3913

Rodríguez Solís, Eduardo.
    Black Jack. In coll. 32/4471
    Ese viejo no es un viejo, es la esperanza. In coll.
        32/4471
    Ruedas ruedan, Las. In per. M, 4, 1965, p.50-78
        (30/3914)

Rodríguez Suárez, Roberto.
    Casorio, El. In anthol. 40/7313
    Ventanas, Las. In anthol. 40/7312

Roepke, Gabriela.
    Mariposa blanca, La. In anthol. 30/3931a

Roitman, Bernardo.
    Pacto, El (Buenos Aires : Ediciones del Carro de Tespis,
        1965; 30/3915)

Rojo, Gabriel, jt. auth. see under Silva, Jaime.

Román, Sergio.
    Función de butacas. In anthol. 38/7202

Römer, Raúl.
    Mari di malpaís (adptation). In per. AC, 5:4, 1967
        (30/3852)

Romero, Mariela.
       Juego, El (Caracas : Monte Avila Editores, 1977;
          42/5997)

Rosario, Agustín del.
       A veces esa palabra libertad. In anthol. 38/7159

Rosencof, Mauricio.
       Caballos, Los (Montevideo; 34/4041). Also in anthol.
          34/4040 and 36/6795
       Valija, La (Montevideo : Aquí Poesía, 1964; 30/3916)

Rovinski, Samuel.
       Fisgonas de paso ancho, Las (San José : Editorial Costa
          Rica, 1975; 40/7304)
       Gobierno de alcoba. In anthol. 34/4040, 36/6790, and
          36/6795
       Laberinto, El. In anthol. 40/7277
       Modelo para Rosaura o la manera de acomodar una historia
          a nuestro gusto, Un (San José : Editorial Costa
          Rica, 1975; 40/7305 and 42/5998)

Rozenmacher, Germán N.
       Réquiem para un viernes a la noche (Buenos Aires :
          Editorial Talía, 1964; 32/4472)

Rozenmacher, Germán N., jt. auth. see under Cossa, Roberto.

Rozsa, Jorge.
       Hambre. In anthol. 34/4040 and 36/6795

Rubens, Erwin Félix.
       Cuando un mundo se viene abajo (Buenos Aires : Emecé
          Editores, 1965; 30/3917)
       San Martín: 1966 (Buenos Aires : Fabril Editora, 1969;
          34/4042)

Ruiz Cano y Sáenz Galiano, Francisco Antonio, marqués de Soto
       Florido.
       Drama de los palanganas Veterano y Bisoño (Lima :
          Editorial Jurídica, 1977; 42/5999)

Ruiz de Alarcón, J.
       Verdad sospechosa, La. In anthol. 38/7183

Sáenz, Dalmiro A.
       Hip...Hip...Ufa! (Buenos Aires : Editorial Sudamericana,
          1967; 30/3920)
       Quién, yo? (Buenos Aires : J. Goyanarte, 1965; 30/3921)
       Sexto día, El. In coll. 30/3919
       Treinta-treinta. In coll. 30/3919

Salas, M.
       Trabajar para el inglés. In anthol. 40/7280

Salazar Bondy, Sebastián.
    Amor, gran laberinto. In coll. 32/4473
    Dos viejas van por la calle. In coll. 32/4473
    Escuela de los chismes, La. In coll. 32/4473
    Fabricante de deudas, El. In coll. 32/4473
    Ifigenia en el mercado. In coll. 32/4473

Salazar Támariz, Hugo.
    Habitante amenazado. In anthol. 38/7202

Salcedo, José Manuel, jt. auth. see under Vadell, Jaime.

Saldarriaga Sanín, Rodrigo.
    Diles que no me maten (adapted from story by Rulfo).
        In per UA/U, 50:196, enero/marzo 1976, p.39-41
        (42/6000)

Salinas, Pablo.
    Maxtla. In anthol. 36/6780

Salmón, Raúl.
    Juana Sánchez. In coll. 36/6796
    Tres generales. In coll. 36/6796
    Viva Belzú. In coll 36/6796

Sampaio, José da Silveira.
    Treco nos cabos [part 1 of Flagrantes do Rio]. In
        coll. 40/7644; also in per. RTB, num. 365, s/o '68
    Triângulao escaleno [part 3 of Flagrantes do Rio] In
        coll. 40/7644; also in per. RTB, num. 365, s/o '68
    Vigarista, A [part 2 of Flagrantes do Rio]. In coll.
        40/7644; also in per. RTB, num. 365, s/o '68

San Félix, Alvaro.
    Ranas y el mar. Las. In anthol. 30/3932

Sánchez, Florencio.
    Barranca abajo (Montevideo : Ediciones de la Banda
        Oriental, 1978; 42/6001). Also in coll. 30/3921a &
        b; also in anthol. 38/7183 and 40/7303; radio
        adaptation in anthol. 38/7291
    Canillita. In coll. 32/4474a and 40/7306
    Cédulas de San Juan. In coll. 30/3921b
    Curdas, Los. In coll. 40/7306
    Desalojo, El. In coll. 30/3921a & b and 40/7306
    En familia. In coll. 30/3921b
    Gente honesta, La. In coll. 32/4474a
    Gringa, La. In coll. 30/3921a & b and 32/4474; also
        in anthol. 40/7303; in English as Foreign girl in
        FIRST, vol. 6, n. 1, Spring '67
    Mano santa. In coll. 40/7306
    Marta Gruni. In coll. 40/7306
    M'hijo el dotor. In coll. 30/3921a & b and 32/4474
    Moneda falsa. In coll 30/3921a & b and 40/7306

Sánchez, Florencio, cont'd.
    Muertos, Los. In coll. 30/3921b; also in anthol.
        40/7303
    Pobre gente, La. In coll. 30/3921b
    Puertas adentro. In coll. 32/4474a
    Tigra, La. In coll. 30/3921b and 40/7306

Sánchez, Luis Rafael.
    Angeles se han fatigado, Los (Río Piedras : Editorial
        Cultural, 1976; 40/7307)
    Farsa del amor compradito (Río Piedras : Editorial
        Cultural, 1976; 40/7308)
    Hiel nuestra de cada día, La (Río Piedras : Editorial
        Cultural, 1976; 40/7309)
    Pasión según Antígona Pérez, La (Hato Rey :
        Ediciones Lugar, 1970; 34/4043). Also in anthol.
        40/7313

Sánchez Mayáns, Fernando.
    Alas del pez, Las. In anthol. 34/4023
    Extraño laberinto, Un. In anthol. 40/7285
    Pequeño juicio, El. In anthol. 30/3857

Sándor, Malena.
    Dioses vuelven, Los. In coll. 32/4474b
    Ella y Satán. In coll. 32/4474b
    Historia casi verosímil, Una. In coll. 32/4474b
    Hombre de los pájaros, El. In coll. 32/4474b
    Muchacho llamado Daniel, Un. In coll. 32/4474b
    Mujer libre, Una. In coll. 32/4474b
    Penélope ya no teje. In coll. 32/4474b
    Tu vida y la mía. In coll. 32/4474b
    Y la respuesta fue dada. In coll. 32/4474b
    Yo me divorcio, Papá. In coll. 32/4474b
    Yo soy la más fuerte. In coll. 32/4474b

Sanromán, Miguel Angel.
    Liberales. In anthol. 38/7175

Santana Salas, Rodolfo.
    Algunos en el islote. In per. RT, 1:3, abril/junio
        1968, p.16-24 (32/4475)
    Babel. In per. UCLA/M, 3:2, abril 1973, p.41-56
        (38/7197)
    Camas, Las. In coll. 34/4044
    Muerte de Alfredo Gris, La (Maracaibo : Univ. del Zulia,
        1968; 32/4477). Also in anthol. 34/4048
    Nuestro padre, Drácula (Caracas : Monte Avila, 1969;
        34/4044)
    Ordenanza, El (Maracaibo : Univ. del Zulia, 1969;
        32/4476)
    Sitio, El. In coll. 34/4044
    Tarántula (Caracas : Monte Avila Editores, 1975;
        38/7198)

Santos, Benjamin.
    Viagem sideral   (Rio : Ministério da Educação e
        Cultura, Serviço Nacional de Teatro, 1974; 38/7569)

Santos, Vital.
    Martírios de Jorge e Rosa, Os.   In per. RTB, num. 419,
        s/o '77 (40/7642)

Schinca, Milton A.
    Chau, todo.   In coll. 42/6002
    Delmira.   In coll. 42/6002
    Raíces, Las.   In coll. 42/6002

Schön, Elizabeth.
    Intervalo.   In anthol. 34/4048

Schwarz, Roberto.
    Lata de lixo da história, A   (Rio : Paz e Terra, 1977;
        42/6379)

Scolni, Miguel.
    Jesús Terneiro y familia   (Buenos Aires : Ediciones del
        Carro de Tespis, 1967; 32/4478)

Segall, Maurício.
    Coronel dos coronéis, O   (Rio : Civilização
        Brasileira, 1979; 42/6380)

Seguín, Carlos Alberto.
    Encrucijada   (Lima :Ediciones de la Biblioteca
        Universitaria, 1974; 38/7199)

Segura, Manuel Ascensio.'
    Ña catita.   In anthol. 38/7183
    Sargento Canuto, El.   In anthol. 40/7303

Sequeira, J. Antônio de.
    Desintegração, A.   In coll. 38/7570
    Resto, O.   In coll. 38/7570

Serra, Silvano, jt. auth.   see under Domingos, José.

Serrano, Martínez, C.
    Corrido de "El Coyote", El.   In anthol. 32/4486

Serulle, Haffe.
    Danza de Mingo, La   (Santo Domingo : Ediciones de Taller,
        1977; 42/6003)

Schand, William.
    Adobe para los mansos.   In coll. 42/6004
    Elección de José, La.   In coll. 42/6004
    Farsa con rebelde.   In coll. 42/6004
    Sastre, El.   In coll. 42/6004

Schand, William, cont'd.
    Secuestros, perros y otras yerbas. In coll. 6004
    Transacción, La. In anthol. 30/3849

Sharim Paz, Nissim.
    Cuestionemos la cuestión. In per. EC/M, 20, verano
        1970, p.131-180 (34/4045)

Sieveking, Alejandro.
    Animas de día claro. In anthol. 32/4424; also in
        per. EC/M, 1:2, julio 1963, p.40-66 (36/6797)
    Cheruve, El. In per. EC/M, 5:2/3, 1966, p.41-53)
    Mi hermano Cristián. In anthol. 30/3931a
    Pequeños animales abatidos   (La Habana : Casa de las
        Américas, 1975; 40/7310)

Silva, Eurico.
    Divorciados. In per. RTB, num. 364, j/a '68
    Grande marido. In per. RTB, num. 351, m/j '66
    Pense alto! In per. RTB, num. 386, m/a '72

Silva, Francisco Pereira da.
    Chapéu-de-Sebo   (Rio : Livraria Agir Editôra, 1966;
        32/4879)
    Desejado, O. In coll. 38/7571
    Romance do vilela. In 38/7571
    Vaso suspirado, O (Rio : Ministério da Educação e
        Cultura, Serviço Nacional de Teatro, 1973; 40/7645)

Silva, Hélcio Pereira da.
    Galho ilustre dos Cubas, Um (Rio : Ministério da
        Educação e Cultura, Serviço Nacional de Teatro,
        1973; 40/7646)
    Olhos de ressaca: Capitu (Rio : Ministério da
        Educação e Cultura, Serviço Nacional de Teatro,
        1970; 38/7572)

Silva, Jaime.
    Arturo y el ángel. In per. EC/M, 3:2, 1965, p.103-116
        (30/3923)
    Fantástica isla de los casianimales, La. In per.
        EC/M, 25, 1977, p.145-171 (42/6005)
    Princesa Panchita, La. In per. EC/M, 1:3, 1963,
        p.125-152 (30/3924)

Silva, Jaime and Rojo, Gabriel.
    Apocalipsis. In per. EC/M, 25, 1977, p.173-195
        (42/6006)

Silveira, Miroel, and Petraglia, Cláudio.
    Moreninha, A. In per. RTB, num. 369, m/j '69

Silvino, Paulo.
    Anjinho Bossa Nova. In per. RTB, num. 343, j/f '65

Soberón Torchia, Edgar and Arango, Alfredo.
    Pepita de Marañón: es mas el día de la lata. In
        per. LNB/L, 274, dic.1978, p.55-92 (42/6007)

Sola Franco, Eduardo.
    Apocalipsis, El. In coll. 32/4479
    Arbol de Tamarindo, El. In coll. 32/4479
    Habitacion en sombras, La. In coll. 32/4479
    Lucha con el angel. In coll. 32/4479
    Mermelada de auto. In coll. 32/4479
    Mujer enclaustrada en el Ritz, La. In coll. 32/4479
    Trampas al inocente. In coll. 32/4479

Solana, Rafael.
    Dia del juicio, El. In anthol. 40/7283
    Lunes salchichas, Los (México : Peregrina Editor, 1967;
        30/3925)
    No se culpe a nadie. In anthol. 30/3857
    Vestida y alborotada (México : Ecuador, 1967; 30/3926)

Solari Swayne, Enrique.
    Collacocha [radio adaptation] In anthol. 38/7291

Solórzano, Carlos.
    Cruce de vías. In anthol. 30/3857; in English as
        Crossroads in anthol. 00/4
    Crucificado, El. In coll. 36/6798; also in per. RCR,
        5:14, junio 1969 (32/4458); in English as
        Crucifixion in anthol. 00/5
    Fantoches, Los. In coll. 36/6798; also in anthol.
        00/7 and 34/4047
    Hechicero, El. In anthol. 34/4040 and 36/6795
    Manos de dios, Los. In coll. 36/6798
    Mea culpa. In per. UV/PH, 2, 43, julio/sept. 1967,
        p.596-605 (32/4481)
    Sueño de ángel, El. In coll. 36/6798

Somigliana, Carlos.
    Amarillo (Buenos Aires : Falbo Librero Editor, 1965;
        30/3926a)
    Amor de ciudad grande (Buenos Aires : Falbo Librero
        Editor, 1965; 30/3927)
    Bolsa de agua caliente, La. In anthol. 30/3861

Somigliana, Carlos, jt. author. see under Cossa, Roberto.

Soria, Ezequiel.
    Deber, El. In coll. 30/3928
    Política casera. In coll. 30/3928

Sotelo H., Aureo.
    Huancapetí está negreando, El (Lima : Talleres
        Gráficos de Editorial INTI, 1973; 38/7200)

Souto, Alexandrino de.
    Bomba, A. In per. RTB, num. 420, n/d '77 (40/7642)

Souza, Jadir Vilela de.
    Neurose. In coll. 38/7573
    Único recurso, O. In coll. 38/7573

Souza, M.
    Contatos amazônicos do Terceiro Grau. In anthol.
        42/6366

Speranza, Rolando.
    Toda una vida.   In per. PRIA, 96, marzo 1968, p.44-57
        (36/6799)

St. Jean, Serge.
    Terre aux fruits d'or, La   (Port-au-Prince : Imprimerie
        Panorama, 1970; 34/4302 and 36/7175)

Steiner, Rolando.
    Drama corriente, Un. In anthol. 34/4040; also in per.
        REPERTORIO, 5:14, junio 1969 (32/4458)
    Puerta, La. In anthol. 34/4040; radio adaptation in
        anthol. 38/7291
    Trilogía del matrimonio, La. In anthol. 34/4040 and
        36/6795

Storni, Alfonsina.
    Blanco, Negro, Blanco. In coll. 38/7201
    Degolladores de estatuas, Los. In coll. 38/7201
    Dios de los pájaros, El. In coll. 38/7201
    Jorge y su conciencia. In coll. 38.7201
    Pedro y Pedrito. In coll. 38/7201
    Sueño en el camino, El. In coll. 38/7201

Strassberg, Sara.
    Sócrates   (Buenos Aires : Ismael B. Colombo Editor,
        1971; 36/6800)

Suárez Figueroa, Sergio.
    Peste negra, La   (La Paz : Univ. Mayor de San Andrés,
        Centro de Estudiantes, Facultad de Filosofía y
        Letras, 1967; 30/3930)

Suarez Radillo, Carlos Miguel.
    Temas y estilos [radio adaptation] In anthol. 38/7291

Suassuna, Ariano.
    Casamento suspeitoso, O. In coll. 38/7576
    Farsa da boa preguiça   (Rio : Livraria José Olympio
        Editora, 1974; 38/7574)
    Mulher vestida de sol, Uma   (Recife : Imprensa
        Universitária, 1964; 30/4212)
    Pena e a lei, A   (Rio : Livraria Agir Editora, 1971;
        38/7575)

Taibo, Francisco Ignacio.
    Cazadores, Los   (México : Rafael Peregrina Editor, 1965;
        30/3931)

Talesnik, Ricardo.
    Cien veces no debo   (Buenos Aires : Talía, 1972;
        40/7311)
    Fiaca, La   (Buenos Aires : Talía, 1967; 32/4482)

Talesnik, Ricardo, jt. auth. see under Cossa, Roberto.

Tálice, Roberto A. and Montaine, Eliseo.
    Swing para una rosa de luto   (Buenos Aires : Ediciones
        del Carro de Tespis, 1967; 32/4483)

Tamayo, J.
    Traviata; o, La morena de las clavellinas.   In anthol.
        40/7280

Tapia y Rivera, Alejandro.
    Bernardo de Palissy   (Barcelona : Ediciones Rumbos, 1967;
        32/4484 and Barcelona : Editorial Vosgos, 1977;
        42/6008).   Also in coll. 34/4050
    Camoens.   In coll. 34/4049 and 34/4050
    Cuarterona, La.   In coll. 34/4050; also in anthol.
        40/7312
    Hero.   In coll. 34/4049 and 34/4050

Tobar García, Francisco., cont'd
    Extraña ocupación.   In coll. 32/4487
    Sobras para el gusano.   In anthol. 34/4047

Tojeiro, Gastão.
    Simpático Jeremias, O.   In per. RTB, num. 350, m/a '66

Torres, Fielden.
    Tribunal, El.   In anthol. 38/7202

Torres Molina, Susana.
    Extraña juguete   (Buenos Aires : Editorial Apex, 1978;
        42/6012

Torres Pita, Carlos.
    Definición, La   (La Habana : Unión de Escritores y
        Artistas de Cuba; 1971; 36/6802)

Torres, Víctor.
    Casa en lota alto, Una   (La Habana : Casa de las
        Américas, 1973; 38/7205)

Torroella, Alfredo.
    Mulato, El.   In anthol. 42/6010

Toscano, Carmen.
    Llorona, La.   In anthol. 38/7206

Tourinho, Nazareno.
    Severa romana (Belém : Govêrno do Estado do Pará,
        1970; 38/7577)

Tovar, Juan.
    Coloquio de la rueda y su centro (Monterrey : Ediciones
        Sierra Madre, 1970; 32/4488)
    Markheim. In anthol. 38/7161; also in per. UNAM/UM,
        25:11, julio 1971 (36/6803)

Tovar, Juan; Vinos, Ricardo; and García Saldaña, Parménides.
    Pueblo fantasma. In per. UV/PH, 11:41, enero/marzo
        1967, p.149-175 (32/4489)

TPB.
    I took Panamá. In anthol. 42/6011

Trejo, Nemesio.
    Mujeres lindas, Las. In anthol. 00/1
    Oleos de chico, Los. In anthol. 00/1

Triana, José.
    Mayor general hablará de teogonía, El. In anthol.
        00/7 and 30/3886
    Noche de los asesinos, La. In anthol. 42/5986; also
        in per. TDR, 14:2, winter 1970, in English
        (32/4490); in English as Criminals in anthol. 00/9

Trouillot, Henock.
    Dessalines ou le Sang du Pont-Rouge (Port-au-Prince :
        Imprimerie des Antilles, 1967; 34/4303)

Trujillo, Manuel.
    Avaricia. In anthol. 42/6013
    Gentilmuerto, El. In coll. 00/6
    Movilización general. In coll. 00/6

Uriz, Francisco, jt. auth. see under Diaz, Jorge.

Urondo, Francisco.
    Archivo General de Indias. In coll. 34/4052
    Homenaje a Dumas. In coll. 34/4052
    Muchas felicidades. In coll. 34/4052
    Sainete con variaciones. In coll. 34/4052; also in
        anthol. 30/3861
    Veraneando. In per. CDLA/CO, 3:7, abril 1968, p.26-68
        (34/4053)

Urquizo, Francisco L.
    Fui soldado de levita. In anthol. 38/7206

Urquizo Huici, Carlos Fernando.
    Paranoia (La Paz : Comité Cívico Paceño, 1978;
        42/6014)

Urruty, Esteban.
    Aguas sucias, Las   (Buenos Aires : Editorial Talía,
        1967; 32/4491)

Urueta, Margarita.
    Confesiones de Sor Juana Inés de la Cruz.   In anthol.
        36/6780
    Hombre y su máscara, El.   In anthol. 30/3889a
    Señor Perro, El.   In anthol. 34/4023

Usigli, Rodolfo.
    Buenos días, Señor Presidente!   (México : Editorial
        Joaquín Mortiz, 1972; 36/6804)
    Caso Flores, El.   In per. CAM, 6, 1971, p.205-232
        (36/6805)
    Corona de luz.   In anthol. 34/4023
    Corona de sombra.   In anthol. 42/5986
    Encuentro, El.   In coll. 30/3935
    Gesticulador, El.   In anthol. 38/7183
    Gran circo del mundo, El.   In per. CAM, 28:2,
        marzo/abril 1969, p.38-96 (38/7207)
    Navío cargado, Un.   In coll. 30/3935
    Testamento y el viudo, El.   In coll. 30/3935
    Vacaciones II.   In anthol. 30/3857
    Viejos, Los.   In anthol. 36/6806

Uslar Braun, Arturo.
    Otro Cristo, El.   In coll. 42/6015
    Silencio del Señor, El.   In coll. 42/6015
    Zorro de seda Talleyrand, El.   In coll. 42/6015

Vacarezza, Alberto.
    Barrio norte   (Buenos Aires : Ediciones del Carro de
        Tespis, 1969; 36/6807

Vadell, Jaime;   Salcedo, José Manuel; and Benavente P., David.
    Bienaventurados los pobres   (Santiago : Ediciones
        Aconcagua, 1978; 42/6016

Valdés Vivó, Raúl.
    Naranjas en Saigón   (La Habana : Editorial Arte y
        Literatura, 1977; 42/6017).   Also in per. COLA/CO,
        12, enero/abril 1972, p.26-56 (36/6808)

Valerio, J. F.
    Perro huevero aunque le quemen el hocico.   In anthol.
        40/7280

Valle Filho, Esmerino Ribeiro do.
    Julgamento de uma freira   (Belo Horizonte : Imprensa
        Oficial, 1974; 42/6382)

Vallejo, César Abraham.
    Colacho hermanos o Presidentes de América.   In coll.
        42/6018

Vallejo, César Abraham, cont'd.
    Entre las dos orillas corre el río. In coll.
        42/6018
    Lock-out. In coll. 42/6018
    Piedra cansada, La. In coll. 42/6018

Valluzi, José.
    Três peraltas na praça. In per. RTB, num. 384,
        nov./dez. 1971 (38/7565)

Vanegas Arroyo, Antonio.
    México 1900. In anthol. 32/4486

Varela, Cruz.
    Dido. In anthol. 40/7303

Veiga, Pedro.
    Circo rataplan, O. In per. RTB, num 425, s/o '78
        (40/7642)

Velásquez, G.
    Ahí vienen los aleluyas. In anthol. 34/3996 and
        38/7161

Veloz Maggiolo, Marcio.
    Creonte. In coll. 30/3266

Viana, O.
    Cuatro cuadras de tierra. In anthol. 34/4046

Vianna Filho, Oduvaldo.
    Corpo a corpo. In per RTB, num. 387, m/j '72
    Matador. In per RTB, num. 346, j/a '65
Vianna Filho, Oduvaldo and Gullar, Ferreira.
    Se correr o bicho pega, se ficar o bicho come   (Rio :
        Civilização Brasileira, 1966; 32/4880)

Vianna, Oduvaldo.
    Castagnaro de festa, O. In per. RTB, num. 361, j/f
        '68

Vicente, José.
    Assalto, O. In per. RTB, num. 375, m/j '70
    Hoje é dia de rock   (Rio : Lia, 1972; 40/7647)

Vieira, César.
    Evangelho segundo Zebedeu, O. In per. RTB, num. 404,
        m/a '75 (40/7642)
    Rei momo. In per. RTB, num. 411, m/j '76 (40/7642)

Vilalta, Maruxa.
    9, El (México : Editorial Ecuador, 1966; 32/4493);
        radio adaptation in anthol. 38/7291
    Cuestión de narices (México : UNAM, 1967; 32/4492).
        Also in coll. 34/4054 and 34/4056; also in
        anthol. 34/4023 and 34/4040

Vilalta, Maruxa, cont'd.
  Desorientados, Los. In coll. 34/4056
  Día loco, Un. In coll. 34/4054 and 34/4056; in French
      as Jour de folie in PLAISIR, num. 369, j/a '69
  Esta noche juntos, amandonos tanto (México : OPIC,
      1970; 34/4055). Also in coll. 34/4056; also in
      anthol. 40/7284
  Historia de El (México : UNAM, Difusión Cultural,
      Departamento de Teatro, 1979; 42/6019)
  Nada como el piso (México : Joaquín Mortiz, 1977;
      40/7316)
  País feliz, Un (México : Editorial Ecuador, 1965;
      32/4494). Also in coll. 34/4054 and 34/4056;
      also in anthol. 30/3889a
  Soliloquio del tiempo. In coll. 34/4054 and 34/4056
  Última letra, La. In coll. 34/4054 and 34/4056

Villafañe, Javier.
  La calle de los fantasmas. In per. CDLA/CO, 24,
      abril/junio 1975 (40/7255)

Villaurrutia, Xavier.
  Ausente, El. In coll. 30/3936
  En qué piensas? In coll. 30/3936
  Ha llegado el momento. In coll. 30/3936
  Hiedra, La. In coll. 30/3936
  Invitación a la muerte. In coll. 30/3936; also in
      anthol. 42/5986
  Juego peligrosos. In coll. 30/3936
  Mujer legítima, La. In coll. 30/3936
  Mulata de Córdoba, La. In coll. 30/3936
  Parece mentira. In coll. 30/3936; also in anthol.
      38/7183; in English as Incredible though it seems
      in anthol. 00/4
  Pobre barba azul, El. In 30/3936
  Sea Usted breve. In coll. 30/3936; also in anthol.
      30/3857
  Solterón, El. In coll. 30/3936
  Tragedia de las equivocaciones. In coll. 30/3936
  Yerro candente, El. In coll. 30/3936

Villegas, Oscar.
  Marlon Brando es otro. In anthol. 38/7161
  Paz de la buena gente, La. In per. RBA, 13:18,
      nov./dic. 1967, p.49-64 (32/4495)
  Santa Catarina. In anthol. 42/5990

Viñas, David.
  Dorrego. In coll. 38/7208
  Lisandro (Buenos Aires : Editorial Merlin, 1971;
      36/6809)
  Maniobras. In coll. 38/7208
  Tupac amaru. In coll. 38/7208

Vinos, Ricardo, jt. auth. <u>see under</u> Tovar, Juan.

Viotti, Sérgio.
    Vamos brincar de amor em Cabo Frio. <u>In</u> per. RTB,
        num. 345, m/j '65
Viteri, Eugenia.
    Mar trajo la flor, El. <u>In</u> anthol. 30/3932

Vlademir, José.
    Paulinho no castelo encantado (Rio : Ministério da
        Educação e Cultura, Serviço Nacional de Teatro,
        1973; 38/7579)

Vodánovic, Sergio.
    Deja que los perros ladren. <u>In</u> coll. 34/4057
    Delantal blanco, El. <u>In</u> anthol. 00/7; <u>also in</u> per.
        EC/M, 4:2, 1965, p.32-41 (30/3937
    Exiladas, Las. <u>In</u> anthol. 30/3931a
    Fugitivos, Los. <u>In</u> per. EC/M, 2:3, 1964, p.114-154
        (30/3938)
    Gente como nosotros, La. <u>In</u> per. EC/M, 5:4, 1966,
        p.92-100 (30/3939)
    Nos tomamos la universidad. <u>In</u> coll. 34/4057
    Perdón...estamos en guerra! <u>In</u> per. UC/A, 124:139,
        julio/sept. 1966, p.148-195 (32/4496)
    Viña. <u>In</u> anthol. 32/4424; in English <u>in</u> anthol.
        00/8

Vulgarín, Agustín.
    Noel y los gatos. <u>In</u> anthol. 38/7202

Wagner, Fernando, jt. auth. <u>see under</u> Bauer, Luisa.

Walsh, Rodolfo.
    Batalla, La. <u>In</u> coll. 30/3940
    Granada, La. <u>In</u> coll. 30/3940

Wanderley, José and Lago, Mário.
    Amanhã é dia de pecar. <u>In</u> per RTB, num. 377, s/o '70
    Cupim. <u>In</u> per. RTB, num. 352, j/a '66
    Papai fanfarrão (Rio : Ministério da Educação e
        Cultura, Serviço Nacional de Teatro, 1974; 38/7581)

Wanderley, José and Rocha, D.
    Era uma vez um vagabundo (Rio : Ministério da
        Educação e Cultura, Serviço Nacional de Teatro,
        1970; 38/7580)

Wehbi, Timochenko.
    Dama de copas e o rei de Cuba, A. <u>In</u> per. RTB, num.
        399, m/j '74 (40/7642)

Williams, Paul.
    A toda velocidad (Maracaibo : Univ. del Zulia, 1967;
        32/4498)

Williams, Paul, cont;d.
  Coloquio de hipócritas   (Maracaibo : Univ. del Zulia,
      1968; 32/4497)
  Tijeras, Las. In anthol. 34/4048

Wolff, Egon.
  Discípulos del miedo. In coll. 38/7209
  Flores de papel. In coll. 34/4051 and 42/6020; also
      in anthol. 34/4040 and 42/5986
  Invasores, Los. In anthol. 00/2 and 32/4424
  Kindergarten. In coll. 42/6020
  Mansión de lechulas. In anthol. 30/3931a
  Niñamadre (Santiago : Instituto Chileno-Norteamericano
      de Cultura, 1966; 30/3941). Also in coll. 42/6020
  Signo de Caín, El. In coll. 38/7209

Worm, Fernando.
  Pílula, A (Pôrto Alegre : Editôra Thurmann, 1968;
      34/4258)

Yglesias, Antonio.
  Hormigas, Las. In anthol. 40/7277

Zamacuco.
  Alguacil, El. In coll. 30/3942

Zarlenga, Ethel Gladys.
  Por la calle (Tucuman : Editorial Atenas, 1973; 40/7317)

Plays by unknown authors

Adoración de los reyes. In anthol. 38/6449
Aleluyas para dos desempleos y un tema de amor (México :
    Instituto Politécnico Nacional, 1970; 34/3996)
Baile de las tiras o de las cintas. In anthol. 42/5120a
Coloquio de Doña Garbosa y Monzón. In anthol. 42/5120a
Coloquio de los cuatro últimos reyes de Tlaxcala. In anthol.
    42/5122
Guaxteco para celebrar a la Virgen del Patrocinio. In per.
    GIIN/GI, 9:1/2, enero/junio 1974, p.189-200 (38/7191)
Historia de la conquista de Quesaltenango. In anthol.
    38/6449
Mojigansas [radio adaptation] In anthol. 38/7291
Rabinal-Achí. In anthol. 38/7183
Tragedia del fin de Atau Wallpa. In anthol. 38/6449
Tragedia del suplicio de San Sebastián. In anthol.
    42/5120a
Usca Paucar. In anthol. 38/6449

Title Index

List of Collections and Anthologies

00/1   Antología del género chico criollo. Comp. by
Susana Marcó a.o. (Buenos Aires : Editorial
Universitaria, 1976)

00/2   Three contemporary Latin-American plays. Comp. by
Ruth Lamb (Waltham, MA : Xerox Coa
Fon-Fon e Seleta, 1968; 32/4873)

00/3   Men and angels: three South American comedies.
Transl. by Willis Knapp Jones (Carbondale : Southern
Illinois University Press, 1970)

00/4   Selected Latin American one-act plays. Comp. by
Francesca Maria Colecchia (Pittsburgh : University
of Pittsburgh Press, 1973)

00/5   The orgy: modern one-act plays from Latin America.
Comp. by Gerardo Luzuriaga (Los Angeles :
University of California, Latin American Center,
1974)

00/6   Trujillo, Manuel. Teatro: El Gentilmuerto;
Movilización general (Caracas : Universidad
Central de Venezuela, 1968)

00/7   En un acto: nueve piezas hispanoamericanas. Ed.
by Frank Dauster (New York : Van Nostrand, 1974)

00/8   Voices of change in the Spanish American theater.
Ed. by William I. Oliver (Austin : University of
Texas Press, 1971)

00/9   Modern stage in Latin America : six plays (New
York : Dutton, 1971)

00/10   Teatro ecuatoriano contemporáneo (Guayaquil :
Casa de la Cultura Ecuatoriana, 1971)

00/11   Contemporary Chicano theatre. Ed. by Roberto J.
Garza (Notre Dame : University of Notre Dame Press,
1976)

00/12   Teatro Puertorriqueño : quinto festival. (San
Juan : Instituto de Cultura Puertorriqueña, 1963)

00/13   Teatro Guatemalteco contemporáneo (Madrid : Aguilar, 1964)

00/14   Asturias, Miguel Ángel. Teatro 1 (Buenos Aires : Editorial Losada, 1964)

30/3266   Veloz Maggiolo, Marcio. Creonte. Seis Relatos (Santo Domingo : Editorial de la Nación, 1963)

30/3848a   Arlt, Roberto. Saverio el cruel. La isla desierta (Buenos Aires : Editorial Universitaria, 1964)

30/3849   Balla, Andrés; Roberto Nicolás Medina; and William Shand. Piezas cortas (Buenos Aires : Cuadernos del Siroco, 1965)

30/3855   Brene, José R. Teatro (La Habana : Ediciones Unión, 1965)

30/3857   Cantón, Wilberto L., ed. 12 obras en un acto (México : Ecuador, 1967)

30/3861   Cossa, Roberto M. and others. La ñata contra el libro... (Buenos Aires : Editorial Talía, 1967)

30/3870   Díaz Díaz, Oswaldo. Teatro, vol. 2 (Bogotá : Publicaciones Editoriales Bogotá, 1964)

30/3871   Díaz Díaz, Oswaldo. Teatro, vols. 3 and 4 (Bogotá : Publicaciones Editoriales Bogotá, 1966)

30/3873   Eichelbaum, Samuel. Pájaro de barro. Vergüenza de querer (Buenos Aires : EUDEBA, 1965)

30/3879   Gómez de Avellaneda, Gertrudis. Teatro (La Habana : Consejo Nacional de Cultura, 1965)

30/3880   González Caballero, Antonio. Señoritas a disgusto. Una pura y dos con sal. El medio pelo (Xalapa : Univ. Veracruzana, 1966)

30/3881   Gorostiza, Carlos. El puente... (Buenos Aires : Editorial Sudamericana, 1966)

30/3886   Leal, Rine. Teatro cubano en un acto: antología (La Habana : Ediciones Revolución, 1963)

30/3887   Lehmann, Marta. Teatro (Buenos Aires : Falbo Librero Editor, 91967)

30/3888   Luaces, Joaquín Lorenzo. Teatro (La Habana : Editora del Consejo Nacional de Cultura, 1964)

30/3889a   Magaña Esquivel, Antonio. Teatro mexicano 1964 (México : Aguilar, 1967)

30/3896   Morete, María Luisa. En el vientre... (Buenos Aires :
          Ediciones Nueva Visión, 1965)

30/3899   Ortega, Julio. Teatro (Lima :Ediciones del Teatrode la
          Univ. Católica, 1965)

30/3900   Osorio, Luis Emrique. Teatro, vol. 5 (Bogotá :
          Ediciones de La Idea, 1963)

30/3905   Pavlovsky, Eduardo A. Teatro de vanguardia (Buenos
          Aires : Cuadernos del Siroco, 1966)

30/3907   Pérez Luna, Edgardo and Julio Ortega. Orfeo en las
          tinieblas. Varios rostros del verano (Lima : Teatro
          Universitario de San Marcos, 1968)

30/3908   Pérez Pardella, Agustín. Savonarola... (Buenos
          Aires : Editorial Kraft, 1967)

30/3909b Rebolledo, Efrén. Obras completas (México :
          Instituto Nacional de Bellas Artes, 1968)

30/3911   Rengifo, César. Teatro (Caracas : Univ. Central de
          Venezuela, Dirección de Cultura, 1967)

30/3913   Rodríguez Muñoz, Alberto. Melenita de oro...
          (Buenos Aires : Editorial Sudamericana, 1965)

30/3919   Sáenz, Dalmiro A. Dos guiones: Treinta-treinta
          (Buenos Aires : J. Goyanarte, 1966)

30/3921a Sánchez, Florencio. Teatro (La Habana : Casa de las
          Américas, 1963)

30/3921b Sánchez, Florencio. Teatro (Montevideo : Biblioteca
          Artigas, 1967)

30/3928   Soria, Ezequiel. Política casera. El deber (Buenos
          Aires: EUDEBA, 1965)

30/3929   Sotoconil, Rubén. Teatro escolar: manual y antología
          (Santiago : Editora Austral, 1965)

30/3931a Teatro chileno actual (Santiago : Empresa Editora
          Zig-Zag, 1966)

30/3932   Teatro ecuatoriano: cuatro piezas en un acto (Quito :
          Editorial del Ministerio de Educación, 1962)

30/3932a El teatro en Iberoamérica (México : IILI, 1966)

30/3933   Teatro puertorriqueño: octavo festival (San Juan :
          Instituto de Cultura Puertorriqueña, 1966)

30/3935   Usigli, Rodolfo. Tres comedias (México : Ecuador,
          1967)

30/3936   Villaurrutia, Xavier. Obras: teatro, prosas varias, críticas México : Fondo de Cultura Económica, 1966)

30/3940   Walsh, Rodolfo J. La granada. La batalla (Buenos Aires : J. Álvarez, 1965)

30/3942   Zamacuco (pseud.) El alguacil (Quito, 1966)

30/4200   Bloch, Pedro. Os inimigos não mandam flôres... (Petrópolis : Editôra Vozes, 1964)

30/4206   Figueiredo, Guilherme. Um deus dormiu lá em casa... (Rio : Editôra Civilização Brasileira, 1964)

30/4211   Sampaio, Silveira. Trilogia do herói grotesco. Teatro (Rio : Editôra Civilização Brasileira, 1964)

32/4399   Arango, Gonzalo. Los ratones van al infierno. La consagración de la nada (Bogotá : Ediciones Tercer Mundo, 1964)

32/4400   Arriví, Francisco. Tres piezas de teatro puertorriqueño (San Juan : Editorial del Depto. de Instrucción Pública, 1968)

32/4402   Avilés Blonda, Máximo. Teatro (Santo Domingo : Ediciones de la Sociedad de Autores y Compositores Dramáticos de la República Dominicana, 1968)

32/4405   Benedetti, Mario. Dos comedias (Montevideo, Editorial Alfa, 1968)

32/4410   Castillo, Abelardo. Tres dramas (Buenos Aires : Editorial Stilcograph, 1968)

32/4412   Chocrón, Isaac. Teatro (Caracas : Univ. Central de Venezuela, Dirección de Cultura, 1968)

32/4415   Cossa, Roberto M. Los días de Julián Bisbal. Nuestro fin de semana (Buenos Aires : Editorial Talía, 1966)

32/4416   Cuzzani, Agustín. Una libra de carne. Los indios estaban cabreros (Buenos Aires : Centro Editor de América Latina, 1967)

32/4420   Díaz, Jorge. La vispera del degüello... (Madrid : Ediciones Taurus, 1967)

32/4424   Durán-Cerda, Julio, ed. Teatro chileno contemporáneo (México : M. Aguilar Editor, 1970)

32/4426   Estorino, Abelardo and Andrés Lizárraga. Teatro (La Habana : Casa de las Américas, 1964)

32/4433   Ghiano, Juan Carlos. Antiyer. Corazón de tango (Buenos Aires : Editorial Talía, 1966)

32/4434   Ghiano, Juan Carlos. Ceremonias de la soledad (Buenos
            Aires : Ediciones de la Flor, 1968)

32/4436   Granada, Nicolás. Atahualpa. Bajo el parral (Buenos
            Aires : Editorial Universitaria, 1964)

32/4438   Halac, Ricardo. Fin de diciembre. Estela de madrugada
            (Buenos Aires, The Angel Press, 1965)

32/4442   Helfgott, Sarina. Teatro (Lima : Ediciones del Teatro
            de la Univ. Católica, 1967)

32/4445   Jodorowsky, Alexandro. Teatro hispánico (México :
            Ediciones Era, 1965)

32/4449   Lizárraga, Andrés, and others. Tres jueces para un
            largo silencio... (Buenos Aires : Centro Editor de
            América Latina, 1966)

32/4451   Maggi, Carlos. Esperando a Rodó... (Buenos Aires :
            Centro Editor de América Latina, 1968)

32/4452   Maggi, Carlos. Las llamadas y otras obras (Buenos
            Aires : Centro Editor de América Latina, 1968)

32/4455   Martínez Payva, Claudio. Ya tiene comisario el
            pueblo... (Buenos Aires : Editorial Astral, 1968)

32/4457   Montaña, Antonio. Tobías y el ángel y El tiempo de
            la trompeta (Bogotá : Editorial Revista Colombiana,
            1967)

32/4459   Obras breves del teatro costarricense, vol. 1 (San
            José : Editorial Costa Rica, 1969)

32/4460   Palant, Pablo. María de los dos y El piano y otros
            juegos (Buenos Aires : Ediciones del Carro de Tespis,
            1968)

32/4461   Parrado, Gloria. Teatro (La Habana : Cuadernos
            Unión, 1966)

32/4465   Portocarrero, Elena. La corcova. Hoy no mañana
            tampoco (Lima : Ediciones Caballo de Troya, 1966)

32/4471   Rodríguez Solís, Eduardo. Black Jack y otra farsa
            (México : Instituto Nacional de la Juventud Mexicana,
            1968)

32/4473   Salazar Bondy, Sebastián. Comedias y juguetes (Lima
            : Francisco Moncloa Editores, 1967)

32/4474   Sánchez, Florencio. M'hijo el dotor. La gringa
            (Buenos Aires : Editorial Plus Ultra, 1965)

32/4474a   Sánchez, Florencio. Obras completas (Buenos Aires :
            Editorial Schapire, 1968)

32/4474b   Sándor, Malena. Teatro completo (Buenos Aires :
            Editorial Talía, 1969)

32/4479   Sola Franco, Eduardo. Teatro (Guayaquil : Editorial
            de la Casa de la Cultura Ecuatoriana, 1969)

32/4480   Solana, Rafael. El día del juicio. Tres desenlaces
            (México : Ediciones Oasis, 1967)

32/4485   Teatro puertorriqueño: noveno festival (San Juan :
            Instituto de Cultura Puertorriqueña, 1968)

32/4486   El Teatro Trashumante: las obras (México : Instituto
            Nacional de Bellas Artes, 1966)

32/4487   Tobar García, Francisco. Tres piezas de teatro
            (Quito : Casa de la Cultura Ecuatoriana, 1967)

32/4861   Ayala, Walmir. Chico Rei. A Salamanca do Jarau (Rio
            : Editôra Civilização Brasileira, 1965)

32/4862   Ayala, Walmir. Nosso filho vai ser mãe. Quem matou
            Caim? (Rio : Editôra Letras e Artes, 1965)

32/4870   Freire, Roberto. Quarto de empregadae, Presépio na
            vitrina (São Paulo : Editôra Brasiliense, 1966)

32/4874   Laura, Ida. Hamlet em Brasília e outras peças (São
            Paulo : Editôra Franciscana, 1966)

32/4875   Moraes, Antônio Santos. Rei Zumbi e, A terra sangra
            (Rio : Editôra Leitura, 1965)

32/4877   Rodrigues, Nelson. Teatro quase completo, 4 vols. (Rio
            : Edições Tempo Brasileiro, 1965-1966)

32/4878   Silva, Antônio José da. A vida de Esopo... (Rio :
            Edições de Ouro, 1966)

34/3356   Acero, Julio. Y la vida prosigue... 2nd. ed. (Puebla :
            Editorial Kosé M. Cajica, 1970)

34/3993   Aguilera Malta, Demetrio. Teatro completo (México :
            Finisterre, 1970)

34/3995   Albán Gómez, Ernesto and others. Obras (Guayaquil :
            Casa de la Cultura Ecuatoriana, 1970)

34/3997   Ardiles Gray, Julio. Vecinos y parientes... (Buenos
            Aires : Ediciones de la For, 1970)

34/3999   Arriví, Francisco. Máscara puertorriqueña (Río
            Piedras : Editorial Cultura, 1971)

34/4008   Denevi, Marco. Parque de diversiones (Buenos Aires :
            Emecé Editores, 1970)

34/4010   Discépolo, Armando. Giácomo... (Buenos Aires :
            Editorial Talía, 1970)

34/4011   Discépolo, Armando. Obras escogidas (Buenos Aires :
            Editorial Jorge Alvarez, 1969)

34/4012   Dragún, Osvaldo. Un maldito domingo... (Madrid :
            Taurus, 1968)

34/4013   Felipe, Carlos. Teatro (La Habana : Ediciones Unión,
            1967)

34/4014   Ferrari, Juan Carlos and others. La Mata... (Buenos
            Aires : Editorial Talía, 1969)

34/4017   Fuentes, Carlos. Los reinos imaginarios. Teatro
            hispano-mexicano (Barcelona : Barral Editores, 1971)

34/4019   Herrera, Ernesto. Teatro completo, vols. 1/2
            (Montevideo : Biblioteca Artigas, 1965)

34/4023   Magaña-Esquivel, Antonio, ed. Teatro mexicano del
            siglo XX, vols. 2,4,5 (México : Fondo de Cultura
            Económica, 1970)

34/4026   Marqués, René. Dos dramas de amor... (Río Piedras
            : Editorial Antillana, 1970)

34/4027   Marqués, René. Teatro, 2nd ed. (Río Piedras :
            Editorial Cultural, 1970)

34/4029   Martínez, José de Jesús. Teatro... (San José :
            EDUCA, 1971)

34/4030   Mazzei, Angel, ed. Dramaturgos post-románticos
            (Buenos Aires : Ministerio de Cultura y Educación,
            Ediciones Culturales Argentinas, 1970)

34/4034   Morris, Andrés. Trilogía ístmica... (Tegucigalpa :
            Univ. Nacional Autónoma de Honduras, 1969)

34/4035   Pardo y Aliaga, Felipe. Teatro (Lima : Editorial
            Universo, 1969)

34/4037   Ponferranda, Juan Oscar. Tres obras dramáticas...
            (Buenos Aires : Editorial Universitaria, 1970)

34/4038   Rengifo, César. Los hombres de los cantos amargos...
            (Caracas : Asociación de Escritores Venezolanos, 1970)

34/4040   Rodríguez-Sardiñas, Orlando and others. Teatro
            contemporáneo hispanoamericano, vols. 1-3 (Madrid :
            Escelicer, 1971)

34/4046   Solórzano, Carlos, ed. El teatro actual
               latinoamericano: antología, vol. 1 (México :
               Ediciones de Andrea, 1972)

34/4047   Solórzano, Carlos, ed. Teatro breve hispano-americano
               contemporáneo (Madrid : Aguilar, 1969)

34/4048   Suárez Radillo, Carlos Miguel, ed. 13 autores del
               nuevo teatro venezolano (Caracas : Monte Avila
               Editores, 1971)

34/4049   Tapia y Rivera, Alejandro. Camoens (Barcelona :
               Rumbos, 1967)

34/4050   Tapia y Rivera, Alejandro. Obras completas, vol. 2
               (San Juan : Instituto de Cultura Puertorriqueña, 1968)

34/4051   Cossa, Roberto, a.o. Tres obras de teatro (La Habana
               : Casa de las Américas, 1970)

34/4052   Urondo, Francisco. Teatro... (Buenos Aires :
               Editorial Sudamericana, 1971)

34/4054   Vilalta, Maruxa. 5 obras de teatro (México :
               Secretaría de Educación Pública, 1970)

34/4056   Vilalta, Maruxa. Teatro (México : Fondo de Cultura
               Económica, 1972)

34/4057   Vodánovic, Sergio. Deja que los perros ladren. Nos
               tomamos la universidad (Santiago : Editorial
               Universitaria, 1970)

34/4058   Ycaza, Alberto. Teatro... (León : Univ. Nacional
               Autónoma de Nicaragua, 1970)

34/4252   Machado, Maria Clara. A menina e o vento... (Rio :
               Livraria Agir Editôra, 1967)

34/4253   Oliveira, Domingos de. A história de muitos
               amôres... (São Paulo : Editôra Brasiliense, 1968)

34/4254   Pfuhl, Oscar von. Teatro infanto-juvenil (São Paulo
               : Editôra Senzala, 1968)

34/4256   Qorpo-Santo, José Joaquim de Campos Leão. As
               relações naturais e outras comédias (Pôrto Alegre :
               Univ. Federal do Rio Grande do Sul, 1969)

36/6754   Arce, Manuel José. Delito, condena y ejecución de una
               gallina y otras piezas de teatro grotesco (San José :
               Editorial Universitaria Centro- americana, 1971)

36/6755   Arlt, Roberto. Teatro completo, vols. 1/2 (Buenos
               Aires : Editorial Schapire, 1968)

36/6760   Cantón, Wilberto. Pecado mortal (México :
             Organización Editorial Novaro, 1971)

36/6763   Cid Pérez, José. Un tríptico y dos comedias de José
             Cid Pérez (Buenos Aires : Ediciones del Carro de
             Tespis, 1972)

36/6764   Cruz, Jorge, ed. Teatro argentino romántico (Buenos
             Aires : Ministerio de Cultura y Educación, 1972)

36/6770   Ghiano, Juan Carlos. Actos del miedo. Teatro (Caracas
             : Monte Avila Editores, 1971)

36/6771   González Caballero, Antonio. El medio pelo y Una pura
             y dos con sal (México : Organización Editorial
             Novaro, 1972)

36/6775   Lázaro, Angel. Alejandra, Ludovina y Elvira.
             Trilogía (México : Editorial Finisterre, 1972)

36/6779   Magaña-Esquivel, Antonio, ed. Teatro mexicano del
             siglo XIX (México : Fondo de Cultura Económica, 1972)

36/6780   Magaña-Esquivel, Antonio, ed. Teatro mexicano
             (México : Editorial Aguilar, 1972)

36/6785   Marqués, René. Teatro, vols. 2/3 (Río Piedras :
             Editorial Cultural, 1971)

36/6786   Méndez Ballester, Manuel. El clamor de los surcos y
             Tiempo muerto (San Juan, 1970)

36/6790   Obras breves del teatro costarricense, vol. 2 (San
             José : Editorial Costa Rica, 1971)

36/6794   Rodríguez Galván, Ignacio. Poesía y teatro (México
             : Editorial Porrua, 1972)

36/6795   Rodríguez-Sardiñas, Orlando and others. Teatro
             selecto contemporáneo hispanoamericano, vols. 2/3
             (Madrid : Editorial Escelicer, 1971)

36/6796   Salmón, Raúl. Teatro boliviano... (Madrid :
             Editorial Paraninfo, 1972)

36/6798   Solórzano, Carlos. Teatro (San José : Editorial
             Universitaria Centroamericana, 1972)

36/6801   Bressan, Lindor, a.o. Teatro latinoamericano de
             agitación... (La Habana : Casa de las Américas, 1972)

36/6806   Rojas Garcidueñas, José and others. Letras vivas
             (México : Secretaría de Educación Pública, 1972)

36/7146   Calvet, Aldo. Teatro... (Rio : Gráfica Editôra do
             Livro, 1968)

36/7150   Leonardos, Stella. _Teatro em dois tempos..._ (Rio :
            Ministério da Ecucação e Cultura, Serviço Naçonal de
            Teatro, 1972)

36/7174   Guérin, Mona. _La Pieuve et l'Oiseau de ces dames._
            Théâtre (n.d.)

38/6449   Cid Pérez, José and others. _Teatro indoamericano_
            colonial (Madrid : Editorial Aguilar, 1970)

38/7151   Andrade Rivera, Gustavo. _Remington 22 y otras piezas de_
            teatro (Bogotá : Instituto Colombiano de Cultura,
            1973)

38/7153   Argüelles, Hugo. _Los cuervos están de luto y El_
            tejedor de milagros (México : Organización Editorial
            Novaro, 1973)

38/7154   Azar, Héctor. _Los juegos de azar. Seis obras en un_
            acto (México : Secretaría de Educación Pública,
            1973)

38/7159   _Caminos del teatro latinoamericano..._ (La Habana :
            Casa de las Américas, 1973)

38/7161   Carballido, Emilio, ed. _Teatro joven de México: 15_
            obras seleccionadas... (México : Organización
            Editorial Novaro, 1973)

38/7162   Carballido, EEmilio, ed. _El arca de Noé. Antología y_
            apostillas de teatro infantil (México : Secretaría de
            Educación Pública, 1974)

38/7165   _Teatro dificil_ (Madrid : Escelicer, 1971)

38/7166   Díaz, Jorge. _El velero en la botella..._ (Santiago :
            Editorial Universitaria, 1973)

38/7171   Ghiano, Juan Carlos, ed. _Teatro argentino_
            contemporaneo: 1949-1969 (Madrid : Aguilar, 1973)

38/7175   _Hombres de México y del mundo. Primer concurso nacional_
            de obras de teatro (México : Instituto Mexicano del
            Seguro Social, 1973)

38/7176   Horcasitas, Fernando. _El teatro Náhuatl_, vol. 1
            (México : UNAM, Instituto de Investigaciones
            Históricas, 1974)

38/7183   Luzuriaga, Gerardo and others. _Los clásicos del teatro_
            hispanoamericano (México: Fondo de Cultura Económica,
            1975)

38/7185   Martínez Queirolo, José. _Teatro_ (Guayaquil :
            Editorial Casa de la Cultura Ecuatoriana, 1974)

38/7187   5 obras para teatro escolar   (México : Instituto
          Nacional de Bellas Artes, 1972)

38/7192   Peón Contreras, José. Teatro selecto... (México :
          Editorial Porrúa, 1974)

38/7196   Rodríguez Castelo, Hernán, ed. Teatro contemporáneo
          (Guayaquil : Publicaciones Educativas Ariel, n.d.)

38/7201   Storni, Alfonsina. Teatro infantil (Buenos Aires :
          Librería Huemul, 1973)

38/7202   Teatro ecuatoriano contemporáneo (Guayaquil : Casa de
          la Cultura Ecuatoriana, 1973)

38/7203   Teatro escolar, vol. 1 ((México : Instituto Nacional
          de Bellas Artes, 1971)

38/7204   Teatro peruano (Lima : Ediciones Homero Teatro Los
          Grillos, 1974)

38/7206   Los trashumantes del INBA, vol. 3 (México : Instituto
          Nacional de Bellas Artes, 1970)

38/7208   Viñas, David. Dorrego... (Buenos Aires : Ediciones
          Cepe, 1974)

38/7209   Wolff, Egon. El signo de Caín. Discipulos del miedo
          (Santiago : Ediciones Valores Literarios, 1971)

38/7291   Suárez Radillo, Carlos Miguel. Temas y estilos en el
          teatro hispanoamericano contemporáneo (Madrid :
          Editorial Litho-Arte, 1975)

38/7523   Andrade, Jorge. Marta, a árvore e o relógio (São
          Paulo : Editora Perspectiva, 1970)

38/7525   Andrade, Oswald de. Obras completas, vol. 8 (Rio :
          Civilização Brasileira, 1973)

38/7529   Borges, Durval. Teatro (Curitiba : O Formigueiro,
          n.d.)

38/7533   Cardozo, Joaquim. O capataz de Salema... (Rio :
          Livraria Agir, 1975)

38/7539   Figueiredo, Guilherme. Seis peças em un ato (Rio :
          Civilização Brasileira, 1971)

38/7541   Gomes Dias, Alfredo. Teatro (Rio : Civilização
          Brasileira, 1972)

38/7544   Guarnieri, Gianfrancesco. Um grito parado no ar (São
          Paulo : Monções, 1973)

38/7547   Jorge, Miguel. O visitante. Os angélicos. Duas peças para teatro (Goiânia : Editora da Univ. Federal de Goiás, 1973)

38/7549   Lima, Stella Leonardos da Silva. Teatro em dois tempos... (Rio : Ministério da Educação e Cultura, Serviço Nacional de Teatro, 1972)

38/7550   Machado, Maria Clara. Teatro (Rio : Livraria Agir Editora, 1972)

38/7554   Monteiro, José Maria. As medalhas do herói... (Rio : Ministério da Educação e Cultura, Serviço Nacional de Teatro, 1972)

38/7570   Sequeira, J. Antônio de. O resto. A desintegração (Campinas : Livraria e Editora Nova Teixeira, 1974)

38/7571   Silva, Francisco Pereira da. O desejado. Romance do Vilela (Rio : Livraria Agir Editora, 1973)

38/7573   Souza, Jadir Vilela de. O único recurso e Neurose. Teatro (Divinópolis : Academia Divinopolitana de Letras, 1971)

38/7576   Suassuna, Ariano. O santo e a porca. O casamento suspeitoso (Rio : Livraria José Olympio Editora, 1974)

38/7578   Viana, Djalma Castro. Colcha de retalhos. Teatro (Rio : Ministério da Educação e Cultura, Serviço Nacional de Teatro, 1972)

40/6604   García Ponce, Juan. Trazos (México : UNAM, 1974)

40/7236   Adellach, Alberto. Teatro (Buenos Aires : Ediciones Tablado, 1974)

40/7238   Antología colombiana del teatro de vanguardia (Bogotá : Biblioteca Colombiana de Cultura, 1975)

40/7240   Azar, Héctor. Teatro breve (México : Editorial Jus, 1975)

40/7242   Barros Grez, Daniel. Teatro (Santiago : Editorial Nascimiento, 1975)

40/7244   Beneke, Walter. El paraiso de los imprudentes... (San Salvador : Ministerio de Educación, 1974)

40/7245   Britto García, Luis. El tirano Aguirre o la conquista de El Dorado. Suena el teléfono (Caracas : Gobernación del Distrito Federal, Dirección Nacional de Cultura, 1976)

40/7246   Britto García, Luis. Venezuela tuya. Asi es la cosa (Caracas : Editorial Tiempo Nuevo, 1973)

40/7247   Cañas, Alberto F. La segua y otras piezas, 2nd ed.
           (San José : Editorial Universitaria Centroamericana,
           1976)

40/7250   Carballido, Emilio. Teatro (México : Fondo de
           Cultura Económica, 1976)

40/7268   González Freire, Natividad, ed. Teatro cubano del
           siglo XIX. Antoligía, vol. 2 (La Habana : Editorial
           Arte y Literatura, Instituto Cubano del Libro, 1975)

40/7271   Gorostiza, Carlos and others. El puente... (Buenos
           Aires : Kapelusz, 1977)

40/7277   Herzfeld, Anita and others. Teatro de hoy en Costa
           Rica (San José : Editorial Costa Rica, 1973)

40/7280   Leal, Rine, ed. Teatro bufo siglo XIX. Antología,
           vols. 1/2 (La Habana : Editorial Arte y Literatura,
           1975)

40/7283   Magaña-Esquivel, Antonio, ed. Teatro mexicano 1968
           (México : Aguilar, 1974)

40/7284   Magaña-Esquivel, Antonio, ed. Teatro mexicano 1970
           (México : Aguilar, 1973)

40/7285   Magaña-Esquivel, Antonio, ed. Teatro mexicano 1971
           (México : Aguilar, 1974)

40/7286   Magaña-Esquivel, Antonio, ed. Teatro mexicano 1972
           (México : Aguilar, 1975)

40/7293   Palant, Jorge. Las visitas... (Buenos Aires :
           Ediciones Kargieman, 1975)

40/7298   Peña, Edilio. Resistencia: o un extraño sueño sobre
           la tortura de Pablos Rojas. El círculo (Caracas :
           Monte Ávila Editores, 1975)

40/7302   Ribeyro, Julio Ramón. Teatro (Lima : Instituto
           Nacional de Cultura, 1975)

40/7303   Ripoll, Carlos and others. Teatro hispanoamericano.
           Antología crítica: siglo XIX (New York : Anaya Book
           Co., 1973)

40/7306   Sánchez, Florencio. Teatro completo, vol. 1
           (Montevideo : Editorial Salamandra, 1975)

40/7312   Teatro puertorriqueño. Décimo festival (San Juan :
           Instituto de Cultura Puertorriqueña, 1971)

40/7313   Teatro puertorriqueño. Undécimo festival (San Juan :
           Instituto de4 Cultura Puertorriqueña, 1971)

40/7314   Teatro 70 (Buenos Aires : Comuna Baires, 1970)

40/7315   3 obras de teatro vanguardia nicaragüense (Managua :
           Editorial Union, 1975)

40/7609   Bender, Ivo. Teatro escolhido... (Porto Alegre :
           Editora Bels, 1975)

40/7611   Boal, Augusto. Tres obras de teatro (Buenos Aires :
           Ediciones Noé, 1973)

40/7614   Camargo, Joracy. Deus lhe pague... (Rio : Edições
           de Ouro, n.d.)

40/7623   Grisolli, Paulo Affonso. A trilogia do avatar (Rio :
           Editora Rio, 1975)

40/7629   Lins, Osman. Santa, automóvel e soldado. Teatro
           (São Paulo : Livraria Duas Cidades, 1975)

40/7640   Pedroso, Bráulio. Teatro... (Rio : Pallas, 1975)

40/7644   Sampaio, José da Silveira. Flagrantes do Rio... (Rio
           : Ministério da Educação e Cultura, Serviço Nacional
           de Teatro, 1973)

40/7780   Guérin, Mona. Chambre 26... (Port-au-Prince,
           Deschamps, 1973)

42/5114a   Cabrera y Quintero, Cayetano Javier de. Obra
           dramática. Teatro novohispano del siglo XVIII
           (México : UNAM, 1976)

42/5120a   Teatro en Honduras (Tegucigalpa : Secretaría de
           Cultura, 1977)

42/5122   Tres piezas teatrales del Virreinato (México : UNAM,
           1976)

42/5945   Buenaventura, Enrique. Teatro (Bogotá : Instituto
           Colombiano de Cultura, 1977)

42/5948   Carballido, Emilio. Tres obras (México : Editorial
           Extemporáneos, 1978)

42/5949   Castellanos de Ríos, Ada and others. Teatro
           boliviano... (La Paz : Instituto Boliviano de Cultura,
           1977)

42/5952   Chocrón, Isaac E. Teatro... (Caracas : Monte Avila
           Editores, 1974)

42/5953   Comedias y sainetes argentinos, vol. 1 (Buenos Aires :
           Ediciones Colihue, 1979)

42/5957   Díaz, Jorge and others. Teatro... Valladolid :Caja
           de Ahorros Provincial de Valladolid, 1976)

42/5967   Gambaro, Griselda. Teatro... (Buenos Aires :
           Editorial Argonauta, 1979)

42/5969   Garibay, Ricardo. Mujeres en un acto... (México :
           Editorial Posada, 1978)

42/5970   Gaviria, José Enrique. Caminos en la niebla y otras
           piezas teatrales (Bogotá : Instituto Caro y Cuervo,
           1978)

42/5971   Ghiano, Juan Carlos. Tres tragicomedias porteñas...
           (Buenos Aires : Goyanarte Editor, 1977)

42/5976   López Pérez, Heriberto. Teatro (Bogotá : Ediciones
           Alcaraván, 1977)

42/5982   Montalvo, Juan. El libro de las pasiones... (Ambato :
           Ediciones de la Casa de la Cultura, Núcleo Provincial de
           Tungurahua, 1976)

42/5985   Muello, Juan Carlos. Que lindo es estar casado...y
           tener la suegra al lado. Guerra a las polleras (Buenos
           Aires : Editorial Kiek, 1977)

42/5986   9 dramaturgos hispanoemricanos. Antología del teatro
           hispanoamericano del siglo XX, vols. 1-3 (Ottawa :
           GIROL Books, 1979)

42/5987   Oliva, Felipe and others. Un pelo en plena juventud...
           (La Habana : Unión de Escritores y Artistas de Cuba,
           1978)

42/5988   Ortega, Julio. Ceremonia y otros actos (Lima : Libros
           de Postdata, 1974)

42/5990   Premios Protea, 1976 (México : Editorial
           Extemporáneos, 1977)

42/5993   Reyes García, Ismael. El envés del teatro... (San
           Juan : Instituto de Cultura Puertorriqueña, 1977)

42/5994   Reyes Ortiz, Félix. Teatro... (La Paz : Instituto
           Boliviano de Cultura, 1976)

42/5996   Rodríguez, Jorge Mario. El derrumbe. Los otros
           (Buenos Aires : Ediciones Argentinas, 1977)

42/6002   Schinca, Milton A. Delmira y otras rupturas...
           (Montevideo : Ediciones de la Banda Oriental, 1977)

42/6004   Shand, William. Teatro... (Buenos Aires :
           Ediciones Corregidor, 1976)

42/6009   Teatro César Rengifo (La Habana : Casa de las
           Américas, 1977)

42/6010   González Freire, Natividad, ed. Teatro cubano del
           siglo XIX, vol. 1 (La Habana : Editorial Arte y
           Literatura, 1975)

42/6011   Teatro latinoamericana (La Habana : Casa de las
           Américas, 1978)

42/6013   Trujillo, Manuel and others. Los siete pecados
           capitales (Caracas : Monte Avila Editores, 1974)

42/6015   Uslar Braun, Arturo. Teatro selecto... (Caracas :
           Publicaciones Españolas, 1976)

42/6018   Vallejo, César Abraham. Teatro completo, vols. 1/2
           (Lima : Pontifica Universidad Católica del Peru, 1979)

42/6020   Wolff, Egon. Niñamadre... (Santiago : Editorial
           Nascimento, 1978)

42/6350   Anchieta, José de. Teatro de Anchieta... (São Paulo
           : Edições Loyola, 1977)

42/6352   Araújo, Nélson Correia de. Cinco autos do Recôncavo
           (Salvador : Fundação Cultural do Estado da Bahia,
           1977)

42/6355   Bender, Ivo and others. Entrenós. Teatro (Porto
           Alegre : Editora Garatuja, 1976)

42/6357   Câmara, Carlos. Teatro: obra completa (Fortaleza :
           Academia Cearense de Letras, 1979)

42/6366   Feira brasileira de opinião (São Paulo : Global,
           1978)

42/6372   Guarnieri, Gianfrancesco. Teatro, vols. 2 and 3 (Rio
           : Civilização Brasileira, 1978)

42/6377   Marcos, Plinio. Navalha na carne. Quando as máquinas
           param (Sá Paulo : Global, 1978)

42/6381   Teatro Mobral/SNT. Cinco peças (Rio : Ministério da
           Educação e Cultura, Serviço Nacional de Teatro, 1975)

42/6541   Guérin, Mona. La pension vacher (Port-au-Prince :
           Editions du Soleil, 1978)

List of Periodicals Indexed

Whenever possible, the alphabetic codes correspond to those in the
Handbook of Latin American Studies.

A	Alero. San Carlos, Guatemala. Univ. de San Carlos.
AC	Antilliaanse Cahiers. Amsterdam, Netherlands.
AVANT	Avant-Scène Théatre. Paris, France.
C	Caribe. Honolulu, USA.
CAM	Cuadernos Americanos. México.
CBR/BCB	Boletín Cultural y Bibliográfico. Bogota, Colombia. Banco de la República, Biblioteca Luis-Ángel Arango.
CCE/NAR	Revista del Núcleo del Azuay. Cuenca, Ecuador. Casa de la Cultura Ecuatoriana.
CDLA/CO	Conjunto. Revista de teatro latinoamericano. La Habana, Cuba. Casa de las Américas.
CO	Coatl. Guadalajara, México.
CU	Cultura. Buenos Aires, Argentina.
CV	Cuadernos del Viento. México.
DRAMA	Drama and Theatre (ceased)
D	Diálogos. México.
E	Expediente. Caracas, Venezuela.
EC/M	Mapocho. Órgano de la Extensión Cultural. Santiago, Chile. Biblioteca Nacional.
ET/T	Teatro. Medellín, Colombia. Escuela del Teatro.
EX	Exilio. Revista de humanidades. New York, USA.
FIRST	First Stage, became Drama and Theatre (ceased)

GIIN/GI	Guatemala Indígena. Guatemala. Instituto Indigenista Nacional.
INBA/CBA	Cuadernos de Bellas Artes. México. Instituto Nacional de Bellas Artes.
LNB/L	Lotería. Panamá. Lotería Nacional de Beneficencia.
M	Mester. México.
MN	Mundo Nuevo. Paris, France.
N	Número. Montevideo, Uruguay.
NE	Nueva Epoca. México.
O	Odisea. Buenos Aires, Argentina.
PLAISIR	Plaisir de France. Suppl. Theatral (ceased)
PRAAC/B	Boletín de la Academia de Artes y Ciencias de Puerto Rico. San Juan, Puerto Rico.
PRIA	Primer Acto. Revista de teatro. Madrid, Spain.
RBA	Revista de Bellas Artes. México.
REAC	Revista EAC. Santiago, Chile. Universidad Católica de Chile.
RCR	Repertorio. (Formerly Nuevo Teatro Centroamericano). San Jose, Costa Rica. Consejo Superior Universitario Centroamericano.
RRI	Revista/Review Interamericana. San Germán, Puerto Rico. Univ. Interamericana.
RT	Revista de Teatro. Caracas, Venezuela.
RTB	Revista de Teatro. Rio de Janeiro, Brazil. Sociedade Brasileira de Autores (SBAT).
S	Sagitario. México.
SUR	Sur. Revista bimestral. Buenos Aires, Argentina.
T	Tramoya. Xalapa, México. Univ. Veracruzana.
T D R	T D R Drama Review. Cambridge, USA.
TALIA	Talia. Revista de teatro y artes. Buenos Aires, Argentina.
THEATER	Theater Heute. Seelze, West Germany.

UA/U   Universidad. Medellín, Colombia. Univ. de
                Antioquia.

UCCH/A   Apuntes. Revista de teatro de la Universidad
                Católica de Chile. Santiago, Chile.

UCH/A   Anales de la Universidad de Chile. Santiago, Chile.

UCLA/M   Mester. Los Angeles, USA. University of California.
                Department of Spanish and Portuguese.

UCLV/I   Islas. Santa Clara, Cuba. Univ. Central de las
                Villas.

UK/LATR   Latin American Theatre Review. Lawrence, USA.
                University of Kansas.

UNAM/UM   Universidad de México. México. Univ. Nacional
                Autonoma de México.

UV/PH   La Palabra y el Hombre. Revista de la Universidad
                Veracruzana. Xalapa, México.

VME/R   Revista Nacional de Cultura. Caracas, Venezuela.
                Ministerio de Educación, Instituto Nacional de Cultura
                y Bellas Artes.